CHOICES

CHOICES

A Journey of Faith—Torrey's Miracle

Margaret Berger Morse

One Family's Walk Through a Devastating Illness
and the Faith That Brought Them Through

VANTAGE PRESS
New York

FIRST EDITION

Published by Vantage Press, Inc.
516 West 34th Street, New York, New York 10001

Manufactured in the United States of America
ISBN: 0-533-12782- 3

Library of Congress Catalog Card No.: 98-90365

0 9 8 7 6 5 4 3 2

In memory of: My father, The Rev. Robert B. Berger, and my mother, Frances B. Berger, for their love and for giving me a firm Christian foundation.

My nephew, Robert R. Shock, whose life was cut short by this dread disease; and his dad, Richard R. Shock, whose death was also due to cancer;

As they all live now in the loving arms of Christ Jesus, the Great Physician;

And in fond memory of Dr. Lawrence Burton, researcher and founder of IAT;

And to God our Father, be all the Glory!

Contents

Acknowledgments

There are numerous people who helped us through Torrey's illness and gave us support in our faith journey. It is impossible to remember everyone over a period of twenty years. I thank all of you and ask God's blessing on you wherever you are now on your journey.

I wish to name those in particular who have given me support in writing this story.

Whitney, my faithful husband, who has encouraged me to complete this long overdue promised task to Dr. Burton.

Torrey, who supported Whit and me, and Jessica, her sister, through her own illness, and who has encouraged me to complete this story for publication and for her fine editing.

Jessica, and Dan, her husband, who have encouraged me in this writing and continually encourage me on my own faith journey.

My three sisters, Jeanne Jones, Barbara Shock, and Roberta Buckley, for their support and encouragement.

David and Bess Walkden, on whose computer I did the first draft in 1984.

Helen Haversat, who kindly gave her time to put my rough draft into a beginning formation.

Cynthia Fessell, who has read and edited the final manuscript and has challenged me in my faith journey and in my writing.

Introduction

Many books have been written about children with cancer. Most of them are books about children who have died from cancer and/or related diseases or who are long term survivors, having suffered through years of chemotherapy and/or radiation. They are about the strength and courage these children had as they walked through this devastating illness and about the families that journeyed with them. They are about the perseverance of the ill child and his/her strong will and need to help the family through his/her own illness. Some of these books are about the faith in God that the families reach for and come to, in order to survive the imminent and eventual death of their child. All of these books have been best sellers . . . for many reasons . . . but primarily because children touch our hearts!

Difference and Uniqueness

This book is the story of our daughter, Torrey Priscilla Morse, who was diagnosed in 1978 with diffuse histiocytic lymphoma, an adult cancer that is rare in children.

This story is not better than the others that have gone before it. But, it is different. It has a different ending—not an ending, but a continuance. In this story trust in God and knowledge of his love become an essential, and an alternative therapy is the instrument for healing. In this story, the child,

Torrey, not only survives, but lives a healthy quality of life during her treatment. On October 9, 1998, Torrey became a twenty-year survivor of a deadly aggressive cancer.

The story of Torrey is unique because she survived. It is unique because she is among a group of cancer patients around our nation and the world who have done something different to gain their healing.

Her story is unique because her parents were willing to take a risk, a risk out of love, a risk for her healing, a risk that many others have taken and are taking in greater numbers—that risk of choosing an alternative therapy for their child or their own illness.

Today Torrey is twenty-eight-years old, an active, healthy, intelligent young woman, working in the human services field. She has suffered very little with this disease. Most of her suffering occurred in the first four months after her diagnosis.

This is a story of choices. It is a story of a child's parents' willingness to risk. It is a story of Torrey's faith in her parents and a story of their journey of faith and hers in God. It is a story of God working through others, those who touched our lives and provided support and sustenance. It is a story about the alternative therapy she was given. It is a true and continuing story!

CHOICES

1
The History

I can recall today, nearly twenty years later, the details of our walk with Torrey through her illness and the years that have followed.

This tale about Torrey starts in her eighth year, September 1978. Several months previous to this time, Torrey had experienced several summer colds and generally was not feeling up to par. Her pediatrician recommended a tonsillectomy. She underwent that surgery at St. Raphael's Hospital in New Haven, Connecticut. Within a couple of weeks following that surgery, a strange thing occurred. A small nodule appeared on the left side of her throat where the left tonsil had been. This nodule seemed to grow before our eyes. Within several hours this 'thing' grew to the size of an adult thumb nail.

Torrey had trouble swallowing and I believe might have eventually choked. In terrible fear of what her father and I knew would probably be true, we called our surgeon. Within hours Torrey was back in the hospital for a second surgery to remove this growth.

Test results of the growth, by the pathologist, showed that it was malignant. The doctors then went back and took a slice of the frozen section of tonsil from the original surgery. Apparently pieces are normally saved and tested by the pathologists. In Torrey's case the slice used was tested but the abnormal cells were not detected. The same slice tested again proved also to be malignant, having abnormal cells. The doctors at St. Raphael's recommended to us that we take Torrey to Yale New Haven Hospital, as it was a teaching and research hospital. We did what we were told.

By mid-October 1978, Torrey had endured several weeks of testing to determine the particular type of cancer. These tests to my mind were primitive and excruciatingly painful. They consisted of a chest X-ray, bilateral bone marrow aspirates and biopsy, spinal fluid examination, abdominal ACTA scan, and gallium scan. Skin tests and a lymphangiogram were also done.

Prior to the bone marrow test, the nurse had to give her several enemas to clean out her system. This in itself was very hard on Torrey. The physicians wanted extra bone marrow for research and had us, her parents, sign permission to extract it. If we had been told how painful an ordeal this would be, we would have never agreed. I was with her for the bone marrow extractions, and it was horrible for her. We were in a little room. She was on a table curled up in a little ball. There was no anesthesia for this procedure. I remember her screaming as they used an instrument which was a drill-like screwdriver that would suck the bone marrow out of her lower back. I held her head, talking to her so as to soothe her. It was terrible. I asked God in my heart, "How can this be happening to our precious child?"

The lymphangiogram was a difficult procedure done on Torrey's feet. A small needle had to be inserted into a lymph gland to put a dye into the lymphatic system. Then pictures would be taken. The pictures would tell the doctors whether there were any cancer cells in that system, particularly in her liver. The technician had to give Torrey several needles in her foot to numb it, and then cut it in order to insert a much smaller needle with dye into the gland. The technician was not successful on one foot, so she did the same thing in the other

2

foot. Again this procedure was done to no avail. I was there with her as comfort and I could barely watch. In fact, I felt faint and was leaning on Torrey, who was saying to me, "Mommy, Mommy, I'm okay." God, what courage our eight-year-old child had!

Even the waiting period between each test was emotionally stressing, because my mind would wander and tend to be negative. A daughter of a close friend was on the same floor, so I tried to visit her in hopes of easing my own stress. The little girl couldn't talk to me, but I could center my thoughts on her and her family and their needs.

There was one doctor, Dr. Sue Mcintosh, an oncologist, who impressed me. I was told that she had gone through all of the tests that cancer victims go through. She did this just so that she could talk with her patients, not just as a physician, but as one who had experienced what they were going through.

After the testing period, our oncologist, Dr. Diane M. Komp, and a resident intern who was involved, met with us. Whit and I, as parents, believed that both of our girls should be included, though Torrey was only eight and Jessica had just turned seven. They might not understand everything, but we were a family. And Torrey was the one who was ill. It was her body we would be discussing. It was, therefore, essential that we were all there when Torrey's diagnosis and prognosis with treatment were made.

The diagnosis was a non-Hodgkin's type, categorized as "diffuse histiocytic lymphoma," an aggressive adult cancer, rare in children. "This is an unusual type of lymphoid neoplasm to manifest in a child." (Waldron, October 1978).

The prognosis for Torrey was a suggested regimen of two to three years of aggressive chemotherapy and eventual cranial radiation for preventive purposes. Their suggested rate of survival was 80 to 90 percent. But what did that actually mean?

"For years, the American Cancer Society maintained a peculiar definition of a cancer cure as a five-year survival after diagnosis" (Moss, 1980). And this did not necessarily mean living without cancer. For example, among the 2 million cured cancer victims in the United States were included individuals who "still have evidence of cancer"(ACS, 1979). Whit and I didn't want merely five years of survival for our child. We wanted her to have a long life and one of good quality.

Whitney and I were numb after we were given this prognosis. We felt completely helpless. We had no control . . . no way of stopping this disease. What could we do, but to go along with what was advised? What choice did we have!?

Over the next several months beginning on October 25, 1978, Torrey received chemotherapy on an average of once a week at Yale New Haven hospital as an outpatient. This first regimen of chemotherapy was to last nine months. I had to take a day off each week from my teaching position in a local elementary school as did Torrey from fourth grade. Fortunately we were in the same school, A.W. Cox Elementary School, Guilford, Connecticut. Occasionally Whit was able to take off a day to spell me, and several of our friends also volunteered their services.

Torrey received the following chemotherapy drugs: Cytoxan, Adriamycin, Prednisone, Bleomycin, Vincristine, Methotrexate, and spinal pills as an anti-medicine given following Methotrexate. She was given dosages according to her weight and at that time in the late 1970s, the normal routine was to give as much of the drug as the body could stand. Torrey suffered through awful nausea and terrible bouts of vomiting after every session of chemotherapy. We would carry a dish pan in the car for the drive home. Within a few minutes of leaving the hospital, Torrey would begin throwing up.

Whit's cousin, Evelyn, also my good friend, was a great help during this period. Torrey and I would stop to see her at her job at Kneuer's Orchard in Branford, Connecticut. We

4

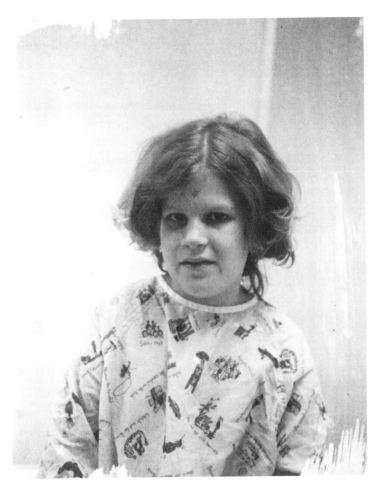

Torrey, age 8, in Yale New Haven Hospital X-ray room, October 1978.

could relax for a bit, and Torrey could use the bathroom before continuing home. Sometimes we made it there before she would have to throw up. She also suffered terrible headaches and bloating from the Prednisone.

In December, we began looking for a wig, knowing her hair would fall out from the Vincristine and/or Adriamycin. I'll never forget the look on the face of the salesclerk. We had gone to Macy's in New Haven. I think the woman thought we were getting the wig for a party. Anyway, Torrey was the one who told her she had cancer and that her hair was going to fall out.

Torrey was seemingly unafraid, at least on the surface. She seemed to comfort the people around her, even though she was the one who was ill. Her hair did fall out . . . almost all at once in one night . . . beautiful golden red curly hair . . . falling out in handfuls in the shower.

It was difficult during those months of treatment to get hold of one's feelings. Torrey's dad, Whitney, is a typical New Englander, conservative fellow; not a person who would reveal his inner self very quickly. He became more adept at this, however, as time passed.

Jessica, our youngest, and in the second grade, was aware of her sister's illness but not its seriousness. She knew that her cousin had died from leukemia, but she hadn't known him well. Whit and I shared that story and his death with them again when Torrey was diagnosed. Jessica was aware of all the attention that her sister was getting, and I am sure she had her jealous moments, as a sibling. Whit and I were concerned for her because we had read and been told that the siblings of cancer children often have a hard time understanding why one child is getting more attention, even though on some level they know there is a good reason. Whit and I tried to give Jessica extra time alone when we could, and our friends and family kept her needs in mind.

I was teaching through these first months, taking care of the family, being a wife, a mother, taking Torrey for her weekly treatments. Whit was always on my mind. He was working full time, too. The strain on each of us because of this illness in our family took its toll. There were days when I didn't think I would be able to function or face anything or anyone. My concern for Jessica and keeping open communication between all of us was on my mind daily.

Torrey seemed to mature quickly during these months of chemotherapy. She had to. We did not hide anything from her and we worked at drawing out her feelings concerning all that was happening to her. This wasn't easy. She seemed to be the one to give us strength. There was a social worker assigned to us, but neither Torrey nor I seemed to relate to her very well. We could feel the sympathy dripping on us as she talked. We did not want sympathy. We wanted hope and encouragement. There was a therapy group offered for family members with children with cancer. This group met at night and in another town, thirty miles away. Whit and I decided not to use this group. Instead we relied on family and friends to support us, as well as the strength we felt from God.

I used the social worker in my school, Jane Preisner. One incident sticks out in my mind. It was a chemotherapy day for Torrey, a Tuesday. Whit was going to spell me and take her. It was in the morning and Jessica had already gone out to the car to wait for me. Torrey was sitting on the sofa, waiting to go. Whit and I had some strong words. I don't remember what we were speaking of, only that whatever it was, it was probably a small matter. But I was stressed and I let all the emotion inside boil up and out at him. I cried and yelled and even tried to pick up the television and throw it at him, which of course I couldn't. Then I resorted to hitting him on the arm as he tried to get away. Something in me snapped and I stopped. Torrey by then was crying.

Whit took us in his arms and held us. I then left and took Jessica and myself to school. I had no idea how I would get through the day. However, I got us there and saw Jessica to her class. I thought of Jane and went to see if she was in. Fortunately, it was her one day a week at our school. She was a great listener and a woman of compassion. Whatever she said got n. ? in a calmer state, and I was able to get through the day. I've al ways been grateful that she was there.

Torrey and I had several intimate talks on our way to and from the hospital each week. Sometimes I felt she was reassuring me, rather than the other way around. She was able to respond to the needs of others quickly. When someone was uncomfortable in her presence because of knowing she was sick, she sensed it and would reassure them or move away.

One of the opportunities Torrey had, which was very helpful to her in getting her feelings out, was with our neighbor Mrs. Reynolds. She was working on a master's degree in art therapy. She called to see if Torrey would like to help her. In so doing Torrey had opportunity to draw her inner feelings and thoughts about her illness. One drawing was very profound. It was a family drawing, which included a mom and dad and a sister. Torrey was there but standing apart from us over at one side of the page. In another drawing she drew a picture of herself with beautiful bright red hair—hair she knew she would be losing. The hair took up most of the page.

Whit and I observed Torrey's faith grow during this time as well. She was determined to be as normal as possible and continue in all of the activities that she was in, such as the junior choir at our church and her Brownie troop. She earned all twenty-six Brownie badges. Soon after her diagnosis, she walked for the UNICEF CROP Walk to raise money for the hungry people of the world.

In February 1979, her dad and I could hardly stand watching this beautiful child physically change before our eyes. Her body was bloated and she was bald. Her sister, Jessica, seven, also watched these changes in her sister. We watched Torrey suffer and be sick from this treatment . . . suffer through the flu and high fevers because the treatment had already begun to weaken her immune system. We did not want her to go through this. We knew all that would happen. A cousin had already gone through similar treatment several years previously, having been diagnosed with leukemia in 1972. He died at age twelve in August of 1974. We did not want her to go through this. We did not want her to die!

At the end of February, we began to look into possible options. What were our choices? Did we have any? Not knowing what might be available, we researched at our local library. We read about Laetrile, Vitamin C therapy, a variety of nutritional approaches, and others. The answer came for us through a conversation with a member of our church parish, Sharon Trotta in Madison, Connecticut. She knew of Torrey's illness, and knew of our concern about the treatment we were allowing her to go through. She had heard of an alternative and told us where we could obtain information. She did not really know much about this alternative, but she was willing to share what she knew and gave us the name of a person we could talk to.

Fortunately for us, I knew the person named and was willing to call. Jay Ferris was the father of a former student of mine. My husband and I went to his home in Westbrook, Connecticut, to hear what he could tell us. Following his lead we eventually met with Dr. John T. Beaty, M.D., P.C.

Dr. John T. Beaty, of Cos Cob, Connecticut, was a spokesperson and support for Dr. Lawrence Burton, the researcher and founder of the IAT (Immuno-Augmentative Therapy) Centre, Freeport, Grand Bahama Island, Bahamas.

2
The Decision

On a Monday evening, March 5, 1979, I phoned Dr. John T. Beaty at his home in Greenwich, Connecticut. Our conversation was brief. He told me that he would like to spend time with my husband Whit, Torrey, and me so that he could give us details about IAT, Dr. Burton, and how he came to know of this alternative method. He also made it very clear that he did not want to talk by phone, and I got the impression that he believed that his phone was tapped. Dr. Beaty suggested that we come to his office the next day. He would cancel his patients for the morning. When I told him that Torrey was scheduled for a methotrexate chemotherapy session at Yale New Haven Hospital, he suggested that we skip it. We took his suggestion, and Whitney, Torrey, Jessica, and I drove to Greenwich. This conversation was the beginning of our journey for Torrey's recovery by an alternative method.

Dr. Beaty gave us his background: M.D., surgeon, and now nutritionist, with over thirty years of experience in the medical field, a member of the AMA, and on the staff at Greenwich Hospital. His involvement with Dr. Burton and IAT had begun in the mid 1970s when his nurse, Becky Hall, had been diagnosed with esophageal cancer and had received radiation therapy, which had caused some sort of collapse in her throat. Becky had learned of the IAT treatment, had become a patient, and was at that time a survivor of several years and in healthy condition. She is alive today and in a healthy state after nearly twenty-five years.

Dr. Beaty had become a support person and friend of Dr. Burton. He began recommending his patients with cancer to the Bahamas. Armed with the information given to us by Dr. Beaty on this essentially nontoxic treatment, our family returned home with some concern about a therapy that was unacceptable in this country, but with hope in our hearts. Time was of the essence. We made the decision, agonizing as it was, within the next week to risk all and try it.

I was teaching full-time and had to get permission from my superintendent and the school board to take eight weeks off. They gave it to me without pay. And Torrey's school gave me permission to give her lessons so that she could keep up her fourth-grade work.

Whit would take care of Jessica, but arrangements had to be made for her to be with someone before and after school while he was working. Whit's cousin and my good friend, Evelyn Linskey, and another friend, Liz Hook, took on that role. The word soon got out to friends in our church and jobs, and family, about what we had decided to do. We had to come up with several thousand dollars to have in hand for the two months of therapy, travel expenses, housing, food, and any other expenses for Torrey and myself. All of the arrangements were made and the money seemed to just come. Our parents had offered and were going to give us help, but money just appeared in our mailbox during that week. A friend from our church offered to loan us a couple of thousand dollars, and did. Also one of my brothers-in-law offered us financial help.

On March 16, 1979, Torrey and I boarded a plane for Freeport, Grand Bahama Island. When we arrived at the IAT Centre that same afternoon, we met Dr. Burton and he talked with Torrey and me at great length. He made it very clear that the decision we had made was risky and dangerous because of the

11

medical establishment's view of alternative methods of cancer treatment. He encouraged us to stay, but he also wanted us to know all of the facts. I felt his compassion and his strength and believed him to be an honest and sincere man. Those impressions have stayed with me through these many years. Torrey became his first child patient.

3

The Alternative Therapy:
IAT (Immuno-Augmentative Therapy)

The treatment that Dr. Beaty told us about is essentially a non-toxic treatment that attempts to control most forms of cancer and one that is easily monitored and administered through a series of daily injections.

The following is a summary of what he told us concerning IAT and its originator, Dr. Lawrence Burton, as quoted from the current IAT Informational Guide.

In 1977, the Immunology Researching Centre, Ltd. (The Centre), was established as a not-for-profit corporation of the Commonwealth of the Bahamas, licensed to treat patients diagnosed with cancer. Using IAT, patients receive injections of sera with naturally occurring proteins to trigger a reaction to kill tumor cells. Thus, rather than treating cancer, IAT directly stimulates the patient's immune system to make a broadly based attack on metastatic disease even in widely separated body sites. The clinic is located in Freeport, Grand Bahama Island.

In 1955, the Centre's founder, Lawrence Burton, Ph.D., a renowned cancer researcher from New York University, began to unravel the cancer mystery. He advanced the progress of cancer research by concluding that many factors influence tumor growth. This observation led him and others to the isolation of naturally occurring proteins found in human blood sera. It was soon discovered that some of these proteins played a beneficial role in the control of neoplastic (cancer) diseases. As Senior Investigator and Zoologist at St. Vincent's Hospital, New York, Dr. Burton's research focused on blood components that keep the body's immune defense system in balance while simultaneously inhibiting the growth of malignant tumors. Following laboratory research with mice, in the 1970s, Burton successfully obtained U.S. patents for the sera, which provide the basis for IAT.

A fiercely independent researcher, Burton was frustrated in his efforts to satisfy the conditions and demands of the National Cancer Institute, the American Cancer Society, and the U.S. Food and Drug Administration. Burton believed in his discoveries, and saw proof that cancer patients' life spans were being extended by this alternative therapy using the body's immune system. Burton decided self-exile from the United States was the only way to advance his work and help people with cancer.

Thus, with private funding, the Centre was established in Freeport. (Note: Dr. Burton died from heart disease in 1993. Dr. R. John Clement, who has been associated with IRC, Immunology Research Centre, since its inception, has continued the founder's work.)

The philosophy of Immuno-Augmentative Therapy, based on Burton's work, views cancer as a whole spectrum of abnormalities characterized by abnormal and uncontrolled cell division. While each cancer is unique to the patient who has it, what is common is a deficiency in the immune system that ordinarily would keep cancer from going out of control. IAT treats the immune system, not cancer, by bringing the body's natural defense system back into balance. The IAT view is that cancer patients don't necessarily have a deficient immune system, but that the controlling mechanism that deals specifically with cancer is deficient. Whether due to an inherited genetic defect or environmental factors, this defect allows cancer to grow out of control. IAT, therefore, treats the competence of the immune system.

Patients accepted for treatment at the Centre are unique. They come from around the world for an alternative treatment that has been proved to extend their lives. While the patient profile over the years has been changing with greater support from referring physicians, the majority of Centre patients are in late stages of their disease with guarded prognoses offered by conventional medicine.

By law, the Centre can accept for treatment only patients who have been diagnosed with cancer. A second screening factor is determined by the variety of malignant diseases that over time have been found to best respond to IAT.

The objective of IAT is to restore the cancer patient's immune competency to a level by which it can control cancer. The body's own complex tumor-fighting system may well be the first, the best, and the last line of defense against cancers.

Other than surgical intervention for localized tumors, there is generally no cure for most cancers. Restoring the immune system to enable it to destroy cancer cells, therefore, becomes the prime objective in IAT.

IAT is not, however, represented as a cure for cancer, but rather a means of restoring the system's natural balance. The restoration of the natural immune system allows the patient's own body to heal itself. The resulting changes can significantly extend the lives of people with cancer, as borne out by Centre records maintained since 1977.

The only true measurement of success, especially for patients with advanced metastatic disease, is life extension accompanied by a decidedly enhanced quality of life that nontoxic IAT provides. A second IRC publication, *Patient Profiles,* describes anecdotal patients progress on the IAT treatment.

Typically, patients presenting at the Centre demonstrate an imbalance of immune components believed essential to the control of cancer. The protocol established for IAT is designed to modulate critical immune factors. By objectively measuring therapeutic progress, the immunologic attack on cancer tumors can be directed.

IAT is therefore a two-step procedure:

1. Evaluation—measuring deficiencies of the immune system, and
2. Therapy— replenishing deficient factors by self-injections of sera.

(Reprinted with permission by R. John Clement)

4

The Beginning Weeks: IAT Centre, (Freeport, Grand Bahama Island, Bahamas.)

I have stated previously how Dr. Burton was totally up front with us concerning the risk we were taking to come to the IAT Centre in the Bahamas. Admittedly I was emotionally drained from the earlier months of Torrey's illness and somewhat fearful of leaving the United States to pursue this essentially unknown therapy. However, Whit and I were at a point where we were ready to do anything that would assist Torrey to begin a journey toward healing and have an improved quality of life during that time.

The First Stay

So, began our venture to the Bahamas. On Friday, March 16, 1979, Torrey and I boarded a plane and flew to Freeport, Grand Bahama Island, Bahamas.

Do you have any idea what it feels like to step into an experience foreign to all you have known? As Torrey and I sat on the plane, all that had taken place over the past five months went through my mind like a rerun movie. I could barely believe it had happened. Torrey had never questioned any of the decisions that Whit and I had made. She knew we loved her and Jes. She trusted us. She knew that whatever decisions we made were because of our love and that we believed we were doing what we felt was best for her. Though I knew that the medical people in Connecticut and some of our family and friends questioned what we were doing now in choosing an alternative treatment, I realized that we had embarked on a great adventure and that it was a positive one.

We had reservations for a hotel that our travel agent had arranged for two nights. We didn't know where we would stay after that. I remember clearly how stressed I was. I had never been out of the United States, let alone in another country with a child. We had to go through Customs, which I had never done. Not a big deal, but to me it was. Fortunately, we met a gentleman in the airport who was also going to the IAT Centre and he helped us walk through Customs and get a taxi to our hotel, which was away from the center of Freeport, near the water. He waited for us and then took us to the IAT Centre to connect with them.

Torrey and I were introduced to Dr. Burton and, as I have already said, he spent time with us telling us about the Centre and the risks we were taking. He obviously believed in his work with immunology and the hope he had to help people with this disease. He introduced us to Dr. John Clement, the Medical Director, a gentle British doctor, and other staff people. We were to come back Monday morning for the beginning of what we believed would be a six-to-eight week initial stay with Torrey as a patient.

Staying at a hotel near the water would have been fine if I had been a tourist. But I wasn't. We weren't. And we needed transportation to the Centre. I was stressed and fearful. Had Whit and I made the right choices? Torrey and I were alone in a strange country that had just recently gained its independence from the British Commonwealth and was in a state of confusion and change. There were burned-out buildings all around us. The hotel we were in was expensive but was barely functioning. Our room had a bed, but no air conditioning, no screens on the windows. There were bugs crawling all over. I learned later that these were a type of cockroach called palmettos and that they were natural to the environment. The only restaurant within walking distance was in the hotel. The food was very expensive. Torrey and I shared one meal between us each time we ate.

Torrey and I spent most of the weekend looking for a place to stay that we could afford. Most places were too expensive or unavailable. On Sunday evening, having not found a place, I felt so helpless. I questioned our being there. Sleep did not come easy. Were Whit and I crazy to have made such a decision? Yet deep within I knew we had made the right choice. Every step had fallen into place and I believed God had his hand in it all. I did not want Torrey to see me so vulnerable and helpless, or my tears of fear. It was she who encouraged me and we knelt down by our bed and thanked Him for delivering us safely to the Bahamas.

On Monday morning we took all our belongings and I called for a taxi to take us to the IAT Centre. In the coming days, we would learn to walk or take the bus. And riding a bus in the Bahamas is not like taking a bus in the States. It is like riding in a small van. Many of them are old and they are hot because they don't have air conditioning. Over the years these became our main source of transportation. This first day began a routine for us that did not change for the nearly six weeks that Torrey and I were at the IAT Centre during this initial stay.

We would get up about 6:00 A.M. each morning, dress, have breakfast, and then get the bus or be picked up to ride with someone to the IAT Centre. We would wait with others for the patient blood-pull. The blood was then individually tested to determine what injections each patient needed for the rest of the day. After the blood-pull, we would go shop or do other errands; sometimes we would skip breakfast at our apartment and then go out with some of the patients and their companions. Between 10:00 A.M. and 12:00 noon, we would go back and pick up the injections to take with us. The injections are given hourly, and must be kept cool. We had a thermos to carry them wherever we went. Usually we had the rest of the day to sit by or swim in the pool at our apartment building or go to the beach or find somewhere to visit on the island. There were certainly plenty of places to go once we searched them out, and places we visited with other people whom we met at the clinic.

We had already spent the first weekend in a hotel, which had cost us a great deal, and I knew that we would not be able to make our expenses if we had to live in a hotel for six to eight weeks. A number of people we met at the Centre on that first Monday had suggested places to stay, and Torrey and I spent several hours walking to these places with no luck. March weather in the Bahamas is not like Connecticut. The climate is more like summer, and we were hot and sweaty after our trek looking for housing.

Bea, a patient at the IAT Centre, and Al Glander were two of the people we met. She was sitting in the waiting area that first Monday when Torrey and I arrived back, with suitcases still in hand, from our search for housing. I, obviously, was very stressed. Bea in her compassion sat and talked with us. By the end of the day, she had had a conversation with her husband, Al. They made arrangements for us to come stay with them in their apartment at Harbor House, a large nine-floor apartment complex out on one of the canals.

We stayed with them for a week. By then Bea had found us a one-room apartment with small kitchenette in the same building. This was a blessing for us. We had a place to stay and we were near the water and the beach. We had a pool to use. We had new friends and other patients from the Centre who lived there also. And most importantly, we had a ride to the Centre every day with Bea.

We met people at Harbor House other than patients. Dot McWhinnie from Canada, and her husband, Art, lived on the fifth floor. They spent their winters in the Bahamas away from the cold just as retirees from Connecticut go to Florida.

Torrey and I would spend time at the pool every day. This is how we met her. She took Torrey and me to the fair at Christ the King (Anglican) Church. She won a chain with a silver conch shell, playing bingo, which she gave Torrey. We have stayed in touch with her and others we met over several years.

We met an English family that lived there in the apartment complex. A young woman with two little girls. Her husband worked for the oil company out on the island.

We met Mrs. Shultz (pronounced Ms. Shultz), a maid for our neighbor, who offered her services and the prayer support of her church.

5

Enclosed Excerpts from a Daily Journal

I have made it a habit most of my life to keep a daily journal. In more recent years, I have kept it on my computer and it is much more reflective. Back in March through May of 1979, when Torrey and I were in Freeport, I had a small two-by-four-inch spiral notebook on which I wrote. These daily notes were written usually in the evening after Torrey went to bed and I had time. I include those from the first weeks and several of the tune-up trips just to give you an idea of what our daily lives, our schedule, and some of my thoughts were during the periods of therapy at the IAT Centre. I even wrote down what we ate.

Diary written by Margaret B. Morse:
March 19, 1979—May 4, 1979

(The IAT Centre is referred to as the clinic in my diary. Shots equal injections.)

First Week

We were up at dawn, 6:30 A.M. Torrey and I shared the last of the orange juice I bought on Saturday and split an orange. I called a taxi which took us to the clinic for our 7:45 A.M. appointment. At 8:00 A.M. Torrey had her blood drawn. It is called a blood-pull here. We walked to the Sea and Sun Manor, an apartment complex near the clinic, to check it out. There wasn't anything available. I felt fearful that we would not find a place to stay. We can't afford to stay in a hotel. We walked back to the clinic to sit and wait to pick up the shots. I was given a quick lesson on how to give them.

We met a wonderful woman, a former nurse, Bea Glander, from Loma Linda, California, who took us under her wing after hearing of our predicament. She is a cancer patient with liver and pancreatic disease. She and her husband, Al, took us back to their apartment at the Harbor House Towers. My fears had been unfounded. Bea and Al have taken us in to stay with them. Their fourth floor apartment has a beautiful view of the ocean.

Bea is talking to the manager about a studio apartment here. We can ride with her to the clinic each day and share gas expense. Bea and Al have been in the Bahamas almost two years, and Bea has been taking the bus to the clinic. She just got the car last week and she thinks it is ironic that we have showed up right now? Is it?

Bea has returned and we will actually have our own place. God is so good to us. I need to trust more.

We called Whit and talked to him and Jessica. We told them about our first day at the clinic and our new apartment,

which will be ready next week. It was so great to talk with them
. . . wish we could hug them!

We had a good dinner of green beans, potatoes, and cheese
with Bea and Al. Torrey is sleeping. I will soon.

Tuesday, 3/20/79

We were up at 6:15 A.M. Al cooked oats and roasted nuts
for breakfast. We went to the clinic for an 8:00 A.M. blood-pull.
Bea and Tor stood in line while some of the patients, unable to
stand, had their companions get in line for them. I sat and
talked with some of the patients and/or companions. After
blood-pull, we walked to the post office and to the grocery
store.

Bea gave us a tour of the area surrounding the clinic. We
came back for our shots around 10:00 A.M. I had to buy a thermos to keep the shots in until used as they are given on an
hourly basis. Torrey has only three today. Bea has eight. She
has more sometimes. I wonder if Tor will ever have that many.
I had a fright when I gave Tor the wrong shot out of order and
had to eliminate the one that was left. Hope I never do that
again!

We had chicken, beets, and potato salad for midday meal.
Tor rested an hour, as did Al and Bea. I read. We then spent a
couple of hours out by the pool. Tor swam. She is like an under-
water fish. Fruit salad and tea for supper . . . talked with Bea
and Al about the routine here and the clinic.

I can't believe that in two days we have actually met some
friends, have a place to live, and are already a part of the clinic
schedule.

Thank you, God.

Wednesday, 3/21/79

We were up at 6:20 A.M. The first day of spring! And we saw the sun rise! Beautiful! Whole-wheat gruel, orange juice, and tea for breakfast.

We arrived at the clinic by 8:00 A.M. Tor had her daily blood-pull, and we walked to the post office to mail letters. We arrived back for the 10:00 A.M. shot pickup and Torrey's first doctor's appointment. Everything is looking okay. We are to check in anytime we need anything or Tor has an unusual temperature or feels different, etc.

We went back to Harbor House and wrote a card for Louise, who finishes at the clinic. We have known her only two days and already feel sad. She is a lovely young Turkish woman married to a British man. She is going to continue drawing Tor's blood in the mornings at her house. Dr. Burton doesn't want anyone else drawing her blood.

I wrote to Mom, Virginia, Evelyn, and Barbara. We had pinto beans with vegetables for lunch; cheese and tea. Al and Tor rode bikes. Bea and I walked to the beach, about a half mile, for a quick dip in the ocean. It was so refreshing! Later when we returned, Tor and I lay out by the pool. The swim in the ocean was marvelous! The water was a turquoise-blue . . . very nice! How could anyone swim in Long Island Sound? Al baked whole wheat bread for supper . . . delicious! We also had fruit salad. Read for an hour after Torrey went to sleep.

Thursday, 3/22/79

Arise and shine at 6:15 A.M. Another gorgeous day! We had oatmeal and apple juice to start our day, and then we were off to the clinic early for a farewell party for Louise. The party was canceled because the baker forgot to bake the cake. Everyone was disappointed. We did errands after blood-pull and bought groceries; a pair of sneakers for Tor, a fantastic buy, two dollars, and went to the post office.

An emergency call came from Florida for Bea. Her brother passed away of a heart attack. They were apparently very close.

Tor and I walked on the beach after doing some letter writing. We went to the pool at the Holiday Inn for a swim, played, sunned on the beach until 4:00 P.M. and walked backed. Bea and Al met us on their bikes. I played cards with Torrey until supper time . . . a feast of lentil patties, apricots, and tea.

Torrey seems to be taking this experience in good stride for a nine-year-old. She has had to grow up fast these past five months. This is a much more relaxing atmosphere and more hopeful. We both are enjoying the climate and beach, etc. Lights out at 10:30 P.M.

Friday, 3/23/79

We were up a 6:15 A.M., but we missed the sunrise. We ate orange juice, oatmeal, and roasted nuts, and drove with Bea to Louise's for a blood-pull. What a precious person! She is going to continue doing Torrey's blood each morning. Her children are here for five weeks from school in England. They played with Torrey while Bea, Louise, and I had coffee and chatted.

We drove to the clinic for the shots. No shots for the weekend.

Hurrah! We went to shell beach in the afternoon. It was blustery, with the wind whipping the waves of the ocean. An exciting afternoon.

This evening I played cribbage and double solitaire with Tor. I wrote a letter to Evelyn and exercised. We had fruit and nuts for supper.

Saturday, 3/24/79

We slept until 7:00 A.M. and went to service with Bea and
Al at the Seventh-Day Adventist Church. It went from 9:30
A.M. to 2:15 P.M. and included a songfest, a Bible study, and
worship time. We met four young adults from Ohio. They
came home for dinner with us and then we took them to shell
beach. The sea was rough . . . really spectacular! Tor and I col-
lected sea glass, shells, and coral pieces. I was reminded of
Schoodic Point in Maine. Tor and Al biked to the beach, and
Bea and I biked home. Everyone took a rest and ate a light supper.

Sunday, 3/25/79

Happy Birthday, Mrs. Richmond! (She is our neighbor
lady at home.) We are going to the Presbyterian Kirk today and
then to the Garden of the Groves. I got up early so as to ride to
the beach with Bea on the bikes. You can find really nice shells,
seaweed, and coral if you go early and sometimes even a large
conch. The native Bahamians go very early and collect them to
sell at the bazaar. While we ate breakfast of nuts, cheese, and
tea, Al and Tor made a hula hoop with the tops of her syringes.

We made church in time for the 11:00 A.M. service. Dr.
Norman Dunning, a man in his eighties, preached a very fine
sermon. I would like to hear him again. How different this
group of people are from the Bahamians we met at the
Seventh-Day Adventist church. Both are friendly, but today's
group was very formal . . . British. We opted to go to the beach
instead of Garden of the Grove. It was great to lie in the sun.
Bedtime 9:00 P.M.

This was our first week in Freeport. Torrey has begun her
first weeks and we have met some sincere, wonderful people,

and we have a place to stay. Many of my fears are alleviated and I am so thankful, God, for being brought to this special place.

Second Week

Monday, 3/26/79

Yes! Torrey and I have our own place! We have used our shells and coral to decorate. I scrubbed all the dishes in the apartment and borrowed several pots, extra towels, and sheets from Bea. We don't know how long we will be here, it is too early to tell. We don't have electricity yet, so we have one more night with Bea and Al.

I gave Torrey a spelling test, and her math and reading assignments for the week.

Tuesday, 3/27/79

I am beginning to master the technique of giving shots to Torrey. She had five today. We have electricity. I took the $120 deposit to the electric company. Torrey spent two hours at the pool, sitting with Dot McWhinnie, a lady from Canada who lives on the fifth floor.

I scrubbed the kitchen and bathroom floors and put the sofa bed together for us. The apartment was pretty dirty, but we are blessed to have it. The rent is affordable and we have to keep a low budget.

I made grits with raisins, brown sugar, and a half of a banana in our little kitchen. We met Bea for our ride to clinic. We went to the post office after picking up Tor's four shots. Letters from my mom and Whit . . . our first mail from home or anywhere. It seems unbelievable that we would be so excited to get mail. But we were!

Torrey has been doing her schoolwork for me pretty well. She seems to like doing it. She gets tired easily, so she naps a lot. We swam and walked in the late afternoon.

I am really pleased that Torrey has decided to get rid of her wig . . . it must be hot with it on. She wears a bandanna or nothing at all on her head. Dr. Burton told her that she should let the air and the sun shine on her head so her hair will grow back, and teasing, he said that it might grow back a different color. I believe they are growing fond of each other. We are both getting some good color. We had an early supper and played canasta for two hours. Bedtime by 9:00 P.M.

Thursday, 3/29/79

I made scrambled eggs with melted cheese for breakfast, with a toasted slice of Al's homemade whole wheat bread, juice, and vitamins C and E.

We took some time to visit with Louise this morning before going to the clinic. We sat in the waiting area of the clinic and talked with other patients and companions. We met three new people from New York, New Jersey, and California. Bea and Al took us to see their friend, Charlie Smith, at the Sea and Sun Manor. Charlie has the same type of cancer as Torrey and is from Ohio. Torrey took to him right away and hopes we will see him and his wife, Dela, often.

After lunch we went for a swim and sat by the pool to write letters. We walked over to Dr. Clement's home in the afternoon, for tea with his wife, Jane. We met their three children who are home for a holiday from school in England. Torrey and I walked back to our apartment by way of the beach. The water was unusually rough.

After a light supper of cottage cheese and fruit, we made bread from Al's recipe in the evening. Torrey had fun kneading it. We had tea and warm bread later.

We have decided to read a Psalm each night. We have been memorizing Psalm 103 suggested by our friend, Virginia: "Bless the Lord, O my Soul . . . " It has been a help and keeps our minds on who the real physician is. I wrote letters to Pat Wyman and Virginia. Bedtime 9:15 P.M.

Friday, 3/30/79

6:00 A.M. get up time. We had corn flakes, bananas, and toasted homemade bread. Ours isn't quite like Al's. I guess we will have to perfect it. We sat and talked with patients in the clinic this morning. I enjoy hearing their stories and feel a bond of closeness with them and their companions. Sharing and listening to each other is a kind of therapy. I find it interesting that the attitude of most everyone we have met is very positive.

Torrey had a letter from her friend Kathleen Hook and I had one from Virginia. She has been a faithful correspondent. She apparently has not received any of my letters. They say things are slow here. I mailed Torrey's two week's worth of homework to Mrs. McDonald, I hope she gets it okay. After we picked up Tor's shots, we went to West End with Louise and her children. There were shops and a large hotel, a beautiful beach, and a huge salt water pool. It is supposed to be the largest in this hemisphere. Tor and I got burned. She went fishing with Tanya and Andrew. Bea and her Jamaican friend, Jo, came too. We had lunch at the hotel; a crunch into the pocketbook. But it was a fantastic day!! To be away from the clinic for a day was what I needed.

I had been feeling lonely and depressed. I felt tears coming at the clinic this morning. Dan, a young adult patient, probably in his twenties, noticed my tears and spoke to me. I guess I am homesick. I feel guilty about my own attitude when I see how positive everyone seems, including Torrey. I am not even sick. Dan is so sweet. He is going home tomorrow. The same flight as Charlie and Dela Smith. We've known them only two weeks and yet it seems like a lifetime.

"Please God, keep them well! Continue your healing in all these dear people!"

Torrey and I played canasta. She won. We made popcorn and sliced apples for supper. Read our Psalm together. We have been here two weeks, six and one-half hours, and twenty-four minutes. How much longer?

Saturday, 3/31/79

We slept late. I got up at 8:00 A.M. and made us breakfast of oatmeal and brown sugar, toast, juice, tea, and vitamin C.

We went to the Seventh-Day Adventist service again with Bea and Al. Al played the piano for Thompson to sing. Actually we went to two services, one in Freeport and one at Eight Mile Rock. We were home by 1:00 P.M.

We ate a light lunch of cottage cheese and tuna on lettuce. We have been trying to eat meals with a lot of protein, because Dr. Burton feels protein is so very important. He has not prescribed any other diet. In fact when I asked, his comment to me was "I am not a nutritionist. Ask Dr. Beatty, when you go home, about what you should eat." We sunned, swam in the pool, and then went for a drive with Bea and Al. They have friends who live in a round house and we stopped to see them. They were interesting and seemed very spiritual, quiet, and contemplative. They live out away from Freeport and apparently don't mix with others. Tor and I have seen the woman walking alone on the beach.

Tor helped make scrambled eggs and toast for supper. We continued our canasta game and wrote letters and Easter cards. Torrey made a mobile for Mrs. Binius, the wife of one of the patients. We read Psalms and exercised on the sheet we had spread on the floor. Bedtime at 9:30 P.M.

Sunday, 4/1/79

April Fools' Day! Whit and I were engaged today, twelve years ago. Happy Anniversary! We slept late—8:00 A.M.

We ate breakfast, took showers, and went to the Presbyterian Kirk (church). Al was nice enough to take us. He and Bea are going to Florida next week, so we will have to figure out other transportation.

The service was quite an experience because a brush fire broke out and as it came past, surrounded the building while we were worshiping. We could see the flames come right up to the huge glass paneled wall windows. Dr. Dunning, the visiting minister, stopped in the middle of his sermon to tell us not to be concerned, because the building was constructed for this kind of happening and that God would protect us. He preached on the Incarnation.

We had a late lunch and spent the remainder of the day at the pool. Torrey worked on homework while I read. We are both getting quite brown.

Tonight we started reading Mark, along with the Psalms,

so we can follow the Easter story in Scripture. I thank the Lord for our friends here, especially Bea and Al, who have been such a blessing to us; for all of our loved ones at home! Bedtime at 9:30 P.M.

Third Week

Monday, 4/2/79

Torrey began her third week of therapy today. She looks good. She is not bloated anymore and her head has fuzz all over it. She has a great tan. We don't know how much the serum is working, but judging from looking at her and hearing her, she seems to be doing well. This is certainly better than all that vomiting and nausea.

This morning when we got up it was raining. This is our first experience with rain since being on the island. It is the dry season and that is why there have been so many brush fires. We even watched one from our balcony earlier this week.

We swam and sunned by the pool in the late morning and walked to the beach. We splurged and bought lunch at the Holiday Inn outside snack bar. The ocean was beautiful, of course it always is. We had fun jumping the waves and building a sand castle. We both fell asleep on the beach and got burned. We took our time walking home. It seems strange to call our apartment home, but that is what it is right now. We made an easy supper of roasted peanuts, cheese, fruit and tea.

Our highlight of the day was talking to Whit and Jessica by phone. They seem so far away. We talked ten minutes. They are fine, miss us, as we do them. Oh, how we miss them! We made arrangements to call again on April 16th. "Please, Lord, bring us together soon!"

Letters came from the grandmothers and one for Torrey from Mr. Kingsbury, Larry. She was really pleased. She had four shots today. We will continue to trust God and the use of IAT as the healing instrument.

Read our Scriptures and exercised. Bedtime 9:45 P.M.

Tuesday, 4/3/79

We were up by 6:00 A.M. eggs, toast, juice, and vitamin C. Joyce Sullivan picked us up to go to Louise's, since Al and Bea are away. We sat in the clinic all morning, visiting with other patients and companions. We met several returning patients here for tune-ups. I understand that they come for a week or two and get shots while they are here. Some go home with shots, some without. Perhaps Torrey will go home without.

There was a letter waiting at the clinic for me from my friend Virginia. It was joy to hear her words of encouragement.

Torrey and I are entertaining tomorrow. Kenny Reese, a new patient from New Jersey, is coming to our apartment to visit, so we are baking cookies. Tor took a nap while I sat by the pool and read. We both swam and then walked. We found a whole coconut branch and put it up as decoration. Tor wants to take it home, but I doubt if we can get it through Customs.

The Bahamian cleaning woman for our neighbor next door, Mrs. Shultz (pronounced Ms.), stopped by again. She wants Torrey and me to go to a prayer meeting with her on Thursday, at the Church of the God of Prophecy. She wants Torrey to have special prayers. I am not sure we should go, but I know I need to be more trusting. She said her church has been praying for Torrey since she first met us. I told her that we appreciated these prayers and we believed Torrey would be healed. I do believe, but sometimes, it is difficult to feel secure when we are so far away from home.

We swam and sunned before supper. I gave Torrey a spelling test and read over a story that she is writing about her own cancer. We played one hand of canasta, read our Scriptures, and went to bed.

Wednesday, 4/4/79

We rode with Joyce again to Louise's, then to the clinic. We chatted with our friend, Mrs. Stuart, from Australia, and Mr. Monroe. I think he said he was from Iowa or Kansas. He is a longtime patient here, and he said he believes the Lord sent him here. This is not the first time we have heard this. Mrs. Stuart is about seventy and has the same cancer as Torrey. She and her husband, a Seventh-Day-Adventist minister, will stay in the Bahamas as long as they can afford to. Then they will return to Australia, knowing that they will not be able to come again. They are living with a native family outside Freeport. She takes the bus into the clinic and he walks in to meet her. They are truly a remarkable couple and full of faith.

I guess we hit the jackpot! There were letters from the grandmothers, Jes, and Virginia. Torrey expressed her love for Virginia. I must remember to tell her.

Kenny came to visit as planned. We had lunch by the pool and swam. She is a delightful and very courageous lady, who has been through a lot of rough times.

Later Tor worked on homework and I reread the mail. I wrote to Whit and Jes. We played a quick game of canasta and read our Psalms and Mark. We want to work harder on Psalm 103.

I am nervous about going to the prayer service tomorrow. I need to keep trusting. "Lord, I do trust you. I trust your love. I trust your power. I trust your wisdom. I trust your dominion. I trust you, God." When Torrey and I prayed, I felt we were supposed to go. In Virginia's letter she stated, "Margaret, you may have to do something that you do not want to do." This had to be a sign of some sort. I am sure this will be a new and different experience for us. "I am apprehensive, Lord, but I lift it up to you. I thank you for whatever happens. I believe your hand is in it. Praise you, Jesus!" Bedtime at 10:00 P.M.

Thursday, 4/5/79

"This is the day the Lord has made, we will rejoice and be glad in it." This is my mom's favorite Scripture from the Psalms, and most all of the letters I have ever received from her start with this psalm verse.

We were picked up at 7:20 A.M. and Tor had her blood pulled at Louise's. We sat in the clinic and wrote letters, chatted with Mrs. Stuart, then took half an hour to pick up groceries before getting Tor's shots. She has four.

We went home to get picked up by Mrs. Shultz and her husband. When they came we had no idea what to expect. We were both nervous, but in a strange way, calm. Is that contradictory, or what? We were abundantly blessed! I am still overwhelmed.

We sat with them and prayed, went through prayers of healing with laying on of hands, and gave our testimony of faith. I don't think I would have gone if I had known we were going to have to stand up and speak. God blessed us today and gave us new friends. We were two Americans, a young woman and child, amongst a whole church of native Bahamians.

It was fantastic!! On the way home, Mrs. Shultz and her husband took us to Kentucky Fried Chicken for lunch. We were home by 3:00 P.M. in time to take a swim and read by the pool. We ate a light supper and worked on our Scriptures. Exercised before hitting the sack. What a day!!!! Thank you, God!!

Friday, 4/6/79

It was so hot last night! We didn't sleep well and then had to get up at 6:00 A.M. We had some extra time at Louise's this morning and later we had time enough to visit Kenny before picking up shots.

Torrey had four shots today. This seems to be her regular quota. We caught Dr. Burton in his lab for a few minutes and chatted. He lets us check up on his mice that he uses for research. He kidded Torrey about her fuzz.

Does God answer prayer fast? Yes, he does! Dr. B. says the blood test shows that there are no cancer wastes in Torrey's blood. Clinically speaking, if I understand correctly, there was no apparent cancer residue. He wants us to stay for two more weeks to see that the blood stays clear. If all goes well, we can go home! I am almost afraid to believe it. "But, precious Lord, I thank you! Keep me appreciative of this miracle, always!"

It rained briefly this afternoon, but not enough to keep us from walking to the International Bazaar with Kenny. She is happy with our news. We celebrated with a rum raisin ice cream cone. We looked for take-home gifts. We swam in the pool, read, ate supper, exercised.

"God, you are good!"

Saturday, 4/7/79

We made pancakes for breakfast. Al and Bea are back, so we went with them to Sabbath School. We shared our good news. They are delighted, but they will miss us.

At noon, we had a light lunch and spent the day at the pool. We visited with our friend who lives here at Harbor House, Dot McWhinnie. She comes with her husband, Art, in October from Toronto, and again each spring, for vacation.

I finished the book I was reading, *The Backstairs of the Whitehouse*, while Torrey was swimming. She is like a fish. We ate supper about 7:00 P.M., exercised, read Psalms, and played cards. After Torrey was asleep, I read my beautiful letter from Whit. He expressed his appreciation for me as a mother and wife. He and Jes, I am sure, are having a happy time together, but he seems to be finding out that taking care of a child and a home is not an easy task. Perhaps there are many blessings to be found in a time of crisis.

Sunday, 4/8/79

After a late breakfast, we were able to catch a ride to the Presbyterian Kirk for the 11:00 A.M. service. Dr. Dunning preached another fine sermon. He is eighty-six years old and in pretty good shape. We had a chance to chat with him and his wife at the coffee.

Mr. Rutherford, who lives at Harbor House, introduced himself to us and took us to a carry-in supper in the evening. We met several families and their children. There was a sing-a-long outside under a large Celtic cross in the garden. We arrived home late, so we skipped reading, etc., and went to bed.

Fourth Week

We are beginning our fourth week in Freeport. I so long to go home. Torrey is doing well, but I don't want to leave until Dr. Burton tells us for sure that we can. I need more patience. I know this is where we are supposed to be. Torrey looks so well . . . it is hard to believe she has cancer and is even a patient.

A patient returnee is staying at Harbor House and gave us a ride to the clinic this morning. We met Bea there. After shot pickup, Tor went with Louise to her house to visit the kids, Tanya and Andrew, while Bea and I went to the International Bazaar. I bought gifts for Jessica, Mom Morse, and Whit. We picked up a package at the post office from Aunt Jane and Uncle Dave.

Torrey met us back at the clinic for her 2:30 P.M. appointment with Dr. Clement. Everything looks good. We expected it to be!

We spent the rest of the day at the pool. We have decided that we need to put in several hours each day before we go home, so that we are really brown! We had chicken and rice for supper.

In the evening I went to the ladies guild meeting at the Kirk with Margaret McNab, a lady we met yesterday at the carry-in supper. Tor stayed at her home and slept over with her children. I enjoyed seeing Rose, Mr. R's friend, again. When I came home, I didn't like coming to an empty apartment, but it was nice for Tor to have a change of pace and stay over. I read for a while and went to bed.

Arrived at Louise's home by 7:30 A.M. for blood-pull. We went to the post office, but there was no mail delivery, as it had been broken into last night. We spent most of the morning in the clinic chatting while waiting for Torrey's shots. She had four today. Then we met Mrs. McWhinnie (Dot) at Christ the King Church for the Coffee Morning and Handcraft Fair. While we had lunch, tickets were pulled for several raffles. Dot had one of the winning numbers. She gave it to Tor and let her pick the prize. She chose a silver conch shell on a silver chain. Dot wanted her to have it. (Torrey has worn this necklace many times over the years and we both think of Mrs. McWhinnie and her kindness to us.)

Torrey, Dot McWhinnie, and Mom (Margaret Morse), 1985.

Mrs. McNab gave us a ride back home. Mrs. McWhinnie, Tor, and I met by the pool for a swim and visit. Later Tor and I walked to the beach to lie in the sun and enjoy the ocean breeze. We ate light for supper. Both of us ate too much at the church fair. We read our Bible lessons and went to bed. Torrey is thrilled with her conch shell necklace.

Wednesday, 4/11/79

We thought we were up at 6:30 A.M., but when Bea came knocking at our door five minutes later, we found out that our clock had stopped running. We rushed and made it to Louise's for blood-pull. At the clinic we met a new boy, Joey, about fourteen, and his mom from Alabama or Georgia. He is the only other child patient we have seen. This is his second bout with cancer. His mom seemed very upset. He is an only child. I hope that Dr. B. will be able to help him.

Later we saw Mr. Rutherford back at Harbor House and asked him if he knew of any free apartments that Joey and his mom might rent.

We picked up groceries this morning before shot pickup. Tor has five today. This is only the second time she has had more than four. I shouldn't be concerned; many patients have six, seven, or even ten, and then have to come back for an afternoon blood-pull and more shots. Some even come back on the weekend. It is a matter of individual patient need, type of cancer, etc.

In the afternoon we kept our usual swim and sun schedule. I wrote to Whit, Liz, and Virginia. We went to Rose's for dinner with her and Mr. Rutherford. They are delightful. We played backgammon. We came home late. Bed at 10:30 P.M.

Thursday, 4/12/79

We tried to get in touch with Joey and his mom at the clinic this morning, but I guess we missed them. All the stores will be closed for the Easter weekend, so we picked up a few groceries. In our mail we had a card from Whit and Jes and a packet of cards from Tor's fourth grade class. We enjoyed looking at them. Her homework has not arrived in the States.

Torrey had five shots again today. This is the third time. I wonder why?

We sunned, tanned, and napped. Then we had a late lunch, including eggs, toast, apple, and tea. I read while Tor went up on the fifth floor to visit the two little English girls.

I cooked fried chicken and french fries, as a treat for supper. Tor did her homework and we read the Psalms. Early to bed.

Friday, 4/13/79

Blood-pull at the clinic today and for the next three days. We talked with Mrs. Stuart and Mrs. Binius. Torrey liked Mrs. Binius's hat. She and her husband are neat. He is the patient. She recommended that I keep a follow-up on the treatment and have blood work done at home. I would think we would do that anyway. Tor was pleased because she had only three shots today.

We were given a TV today from Jerry, our friend on the ninth floor. She has a place on Fisher's Island off Rhode Island.

Torrey took an hour and a half nap, so we could stay up and watch a movie about two mentally handicapped adults who want to marry. It was well done; very moving. We made popcorn and drank apple juice. We hit the sack at 11:15 P.M.

P.S. This morning while at the clinic we stood outside and watched a Friday Vigil procession of the Cross, Bahamian men carrying the cross and a band playing as they marched down the main street into the yard of Christ the King Anglican Church. There was a short service for Good Friday. Very impressive!

Saturday, 4/14/79

It is the weekend. No blood-pull or shots, so we stayed in bed until 8:00 A.M. and ate a leisurely breakfast on our little balcony. Bea and Al picked us up for Sabbath school. There was a very interesting discussion on the Second Coming of Christ. We didn't stay for the worship, as Bea wasn't feeling well.

Dot McWhinnie sat by me at the pool and visited while Tor swam. We will both miss this beautiful pool when we go home.

We made a picnic lunch and walked to the beach. We built another sand castle, the largest yet. We played three games of shuffleboard at the Holiday Inn and decided to stay and eat at the outside snack bar.

Tonight we watched *The Love Boat*, read our Scriptures, and exercised.

I am tired of listening to the music from across the canal. They seem to know only three numbers and they play "Mary Ann" more often than others. Bed at 11:00 P.M.

Sunday, 4/15/79

We were able to get a ride to Christ the King Anglican Church for the Easter Service this morning with a Bahamian lady. The service was from the 1929 Prayer Book. We miss being home with Whit, Jes, and our friends from church on this most wonderful of all holidays!! Tor and I, our family, have so much to be thankful for. "Thank you, Lord Jesus, for dying on the cross for us and for the love and mercy you have given us. Thank you, especially, for the healing you have accomplished in Torrey. We believe it will soon be complete."

I wonder where Jes and Whit had dinner. Did he cook for the Coxes or did they go to Mom Morse's? Did Jes color eggs? We had dinner with Bea and Al. They don't celebrate Easter as Seventh-Day Adventists.

We chatted for an hour or so and then Tor and I swam and sunned the rest of the afternoon.

Fifth Week

Monday, 4/16/79

Hurrah! We have had fantastic news! Just called Whit to tell him. We can hardly believe it! We are going home. Tor had an appointment with Dr. Clement and Dr. Weinberg and had a blood count done. Her count was the best yet. They said we could go home by the end of the week. However, I called the airport and we can't get on a flight until next Wednesday, the 25th. Tor is disappointed, but it will give her an extra three days at the clinic.

We read our Scripture and thanked the Lord for our great news!

Tuesday, 4/17/79

We shared our good news with our friends at the clinic. Everyone is always happy to hear when someone is going home. We tried to organize our stuff in preparation for our departure. We will eat what we have and try not to buy more than we need. Anything left can go to Bea. I cleaned the oven and the refrigerator.

We sunned, swam, and read. We went up to see Bea and Al after a light supper, exercised, and went to bed at 10:00 P.M.

Wednesday, 4/18/79

We overslept again. Took our time at the clinic to use the phone and call the airport. They may have standby on Friday. Tor is excited. I told her not to get too hopeful.

After getting shots, we walked on the beach and spent the day sunning, swimming, and playing shuffleboard. I will miss the beautiful soft, white sand and the clear turquoise waves.

We watched TV and ate a late supper; read Psalms, and went to bed.

P.S. We called Whit to let him know we may be home Friday.

Thursday, 4/19/79

We took Mrs. Stuart to Louise for blood-pull with Bea. We were late getting to the clinic and missed Kenny. We had hoped to see her, but instead got a ride to the airport to recheck the standby for Friday.

Checked in with Lynn and Dr. Weinberg. Torrey got four shots. We sat and talked with various patients in the afternoon while Bea had a doctor's appointment.

While we waited for Bea, the administrator came out and told us we couldn't leave until next week. I was really upset and Torrey was disappointed. She didn't give a good reason. Both Tor and I were so ready to leave that we started to cry.

Our disappointment was short lived. Dr. Burton came out and said he thought we could leave by Saturday. The whole situation had to do with getting the serum ready for us to take. I called the airport to check on getting a standby for Saturday. There is a slim possibility.

We sat by the pool and ate crackers and cheese. I will miss this island; our apartment, the pool, the beaches, the closeness of the patients. They have become our family. But, like Torrey, I am ready to see Jes and Whitney. I guess I need to get my mind thinking about going back to school and teaching, too. Bedtime 10:00 P.M.

Friday, 4/20/79

I got a ride to the airport to check standby flights, while Torrey stayed at the clinic to visit with our many friends. The airport people won't guarantee anything, but we can come at 12:30 P.M., Saturday and sit and wait.

Torrey was helping Lynn, as she has for several days. I sat and talked with Kenny Reese for an hour. I will miss her. We planned a reunion back in the States.

Torrey went fishing in the afternoon with two kids at Harbor House. I cleaned the apartment and took all the things we borrowed from Bea and Al back except the sheets.

Bea took us to the clinic to pick up insurance forms, not that they will do us any good, a prescription for syringes, etc. Dr. Weinberg wished us his best. He is a sweet gentleman from Long Island. I thanked him for his kindness to us. Torrey hugged him and gave him a kiss on the cheek. Lynn and Rose came out for their hugs. We were both in tears because, even though we want to go, we will miss all of the dear people here.

We spent the evening with Bea and Al. They were our life line at the beginning and have become good friends. They have been our strength and our support while we have been here. I will truly miss them. Tor and I will continue to pray for Bea's continued healing. I gave them our leftover food supplies.

ARE we actually going home tomorrow!!!?

Saturday, 4/21/79

We are on the plane! It is true. This is really the day. I believed that the Lord would provide us seats and he did!

Torrey and I were up at 7:30 A.M. She made us pancakes as a celebration. We cleaned the kitchen and walked up to say good-bye to Dot and Art. Bea took us to the airport to place ourselves on standby.

We then went to the clinic to get serum and see Dr. Burton for last instructions and a printout of Torrey's injection schedule for the next six months. He'd continue to provide her the shots. He reiterated his concern for us once we get back to the States, because Torrey is a minor. He feels we should forgo trying to apply for insurance, because of questions that might be asked. I'm sure that Whit will agree. Torrey gave Dr. B. the shell mouse that she had made using beach shells, rocks, and glue from Al. Dr. Burton actually let us hug him. There is no way we will ever be able to thank him for the miracle that he has been a part of.

After a light lunch, Bea and Al took us to the airport. Thank you, Lord! We were the first people for standby and had to wait only an hour. Several times during that hour, I thought we might miss it, but Tor kept reassuring me. And, here we are!

I can hardly believe we will be seeing Whit and Jes in a few short hours. Tor and I decided not to call him until we got to New York. God, you are so good!!! Thank you! Thank you!

6

Clinic Friends: First Stay

Along with Bea and Al Glander, Dot and Art McWhinnie, and other friends at Harbor House, we established many other lasting relationships in our many visits to the IAT Centre.

Charlie Smith, a lymphoma patient like Torrey, and his wife, Dela, gave us hope and faith in the therapy. He always had a smile for Torrey and his positive attitude was an inspiration to all the patients. He had learned to pull blood and could be found most of the time working in the clinic. You couldn't miss him, in his big straw hat and cutoff jeans.

Kenny Reese, our friend from New Jersey, taught us how to play backgammon and hibachi. We became very fond of her and spent many hours in her apartment. After our return to the States, she came to visit us the following summer with her son, Morgan. We went down to see her, too, while she was in Connecticut visiting her dad.

Mrs. Castleberry and her husband, a brain tumor patient, were from Arkansas. She was a kindergarten teacher. Her sense of humor was a marvel to me. She told Torrey about her cat, who was able to get up on the toilet and flush it. We have exchanged letters and she sent Torrey a picture of the cat sitting on the toilet.

Mr. and Mrs. Stuart, from Australia, were a special couple in their seventies whom we knew, and though we didn't continue a relationship over the years, they have been remembered. Mrs. Stuart had lymphoma. They lived out at Eight Mile Rock in a Bahamian home. Mrs. Stuart got a ride to the clinic and Mr. Stuart would walk to meet her.

There were Dan, Joey, Joyce, Mr. & Mrs. Binius and a number of others whom we were fortunate to have the opportunity to know as well.

Not all of the patients whom we met during this initial visit and subsequent trips have lived. It is essential to state that some people who come to the Bahamas do die. It is my perception that many of the people who choose to come to the IAT Centre hear about it after they have tried the established method of treatment in the United States and are given a terminal prognosis. Some have tried other alternative treatment before coming. They come to the Bahamas as a last resort. Because of this thing, some die. But I believe it is very important to say that many of these terminal patients, once they begin IAT therapy, do not die, though they have been told that they have limited time because of this disease. Some live years with the disease and with a quality of life that is good, even though they still have the illness.

In today's world with more people willing to get second opinions and risk trying different alternative treatments in medicine, the patients who come to the Bahamas are not always the terminal cases.

My own sister, Bobbie Buckley, went to the IAT Centre as a patient in 1992, having been diagnosed with a rare abdominal (Pseudomyxoma Peridtnei of Appendiceal origin) cancer. She had had two surgeries in this country, but she was not given a very good prognosis. She was on the IAT Therapy for four years and in good health, but still living with her cancer. She then found a surgeon in Washington, D.C., who has been researching her particular kind of rare cancer, and she experienced another extensive surgery using chemotherapy put directly into the abdomen with heat at surgery time. This was done with no unbearable side effects or loss of hair.

Bobbie did well on IAT and was able to build up her immune system. This building up along with a suggested exercise program enabled her to go through this new surgical procedure in Washington, D.C. It has been two years and she is doing well. She is enjoying fine health and is living in Florida with her husband, Dean.

There were special IAT staff people, who were a large part of our lives while we are in the Bahamas. Lynn Austin, nurse and jack of all trades, was and has been caring and interested in Torrey these many years. When we first began Torrey's therapy, Lynn would let Torrey come into the lab and get the injections to bring out to the other patients. This gave Torrey a chance to be involved. When we first knew Lynn, she was a very young woman learning the ins and outs of the work under Dr. Burton's direction. She had previously gone to Scotland for medical training. She is one of the mainstays of the clinic. We have enjoyed watching her grow and mature just as she has watched our process of life. She has become our friend, and we have spent time with her outside the clinic.

Lee Malone, a technician in the lab, was always ready to come out and greet Torrey. She, with Lynn's okay, allowed Torrey to come back and get the shots for other patients waiting in the outer waiting room. We have become friends over the years.

Gary, a technician who drew patients' blood in the morning and sometimes that of those of us in the family who contributed our blood, I remember as a quiet, gentle young man, with a good spirit about him.

Rose, who was a secretarial person in the outer office, always gave us her warm smile and caring spirit to encourage us each day.

Louise, mentioned so many times in my diary, was a

Lynn Austin and Torrey at IAT Centre, 1992.

lovely Turkish woman, married to an English banker. She had been a part of the clinic for some time when we arrived. Dr. Burton had insisted that she be the person to draw Torrey's blood when we first arrived and even when she finished working, she was kind enough to continue at Dr. Burton's request.

Torrey did not have much contact with other children, but Louise's children, Tanya and Andrew, gave her some special times. The support Louise gave to us was incredible.

In the early 1980s June Austin came to the IAT Centre. She first came as a friend of Dr. Burton's second wife, Betty, who was also a patient. June became the primary patient counselor at the Centre. June has been a confident and enthusiastic advocate for the IAT therapy. She has given encouragement for the journey of healing to Torrey each time she returns for a tune-up and has become our family friend. She hails originally from Vermont, and this has been a common ground of interest for us.

Summary of Initial Visit/Home Again

Torrey had done well on Immuno-Augmentative Therapy. In the five and a half weeks we were in the Bahamas, she was never sick. Occasionally she tired, but there were no side effects from the serum. Her bald head had soon begun to grow back hair and her bloated body thinned down to normal size. Though we made trips to the clinic every day and Torrey had to put up with blood being drawn and getting shots, the routine of the therapy was fairly easy for her. She enjoyed her time. She met lots of people and enjoyed their stories and their company. She was basically happy. After the first week, she began to respond and within three weeks we knew that the therapy was beginning to take effect. Her immune system was correcting itself and working with the sera to battle her cancer. And,

Lee Malone and Torrey at IAT Centre, 1992.

of course, being in such a beautiful and warm country made the stay more pleasant for both of us.

We arrived home right in the middle of the school system's spring break, which gave us time to adjust ourselves into the everyday life routine. It gave us some time with Jes and Whit to share some of our experiences, though it would take weeks to begin to tell them everything.

It would also be awhile before we realized that Torrey really had been helped by IAT and with a quality of life during therapy that is not usually attained by the established method of treatment in this country.

Torrey and I had brought shots in her thermos to last through Saturday and a six-week shot schedule and serum to last us for the next six months. The next day, Sunday, Whit and I sat down and made up shots for her. I had been shown, at the clinic, how to make them up using the different sera. We were able to make them up by the day or by the week or longer. We decided to make them up by the week and freeze them. We put daily shots in baggies labeled for each day and then placed a week's supply in small lunch bags, marked by the week. We made up the first six week supply in about four hours.

Since I taught in the same school that Torrey attended, I was able to give her the shots at the right time. I would take the day's supply in the thermos and put them in the small refrigerator in the nurse's office. At the end of the six weeks, we went to Dr. Beaty's in Greenwich and she would have blood drawn and sent to the clinic. Another shot schedule was then sent to us.

Torrey returned easily to her fourth grade class, having kept up the work while we were away. The kids in her class were really caring and, of course, wanted to hear about her trip. Mrs. McDonald was very helpful in helping Torrey readjust. My class was terrific. They had become used to a substitute teacher, but they now were able to readjust themselves to my arrival back for the remainder of the year. The parents had also accepted the situation well, and I was very grateful. Those final weeks of school went well for both of us and Jes.

They were as normal as possible with the exception of one week when Jessica came down with the chicken pox and Torrey was exposed. We had been warned when she was on chemotherapy that she should not be exposed because her immune system might be low. In this case we didn't know for sure, but in contacting Dr. Beatty, he recommended getting a chicken pox vaccine shot as well as moving her to a friends' home since it was her sister who had them. We made arrangements for her to stay with my friend Virginia. She did have the shot as well. The needle was quite large and Torrey had to have two. It wasn't very pleasant and she still got the chicken pox. She had a serious case, but without the vaccine, it might have been worse.

I had to leave my class again in May, when my father passed away. He had been ill while Torrey and I were in the Bahamas. When I look back now, and remember how he was able to hold on until we were back, I believe that it was as if he waited until he knew we were safe. He wanted to make sure that Torrey was doing well. I believe it was another blessing of mercy from the Lord.

One of our first family outings after we returned was a drive over to the Connecticut River near Old Saybrook. We drove up the west side of the river, across to East Haddam, and then to a parking area where we could walk and sit on big rocks near the water. We had a picnic.

During the summer, Torrey was in great shape. She was taking shots, but otherwise she was able to do all of the activities of any nine-year-old child. She swam, played softball, biked and hiked, and enjoyed her friends.

Torrey (left) and her sister Jessica, 1979.

We did many things as a family and I believe we had grown much closer through the separation. Certainly our faith had become much stronger and our ideals and goals changed. Where previously we were concerned with future plans, we now were more interested in the immediate happiness of our family and lived more on a one day at a time plan. We also had become more caring of each other and found that we cared more about the lives of our friends.

7

Follow-Up

We continued to go to Dr. Beaty's office in Greenwich, Connecticut, every six weeks for a checkup and blood-pull and to get new shot schedules from the IAT Centre.

In November 1979, we returned to Freeport for the six-month checkup (tune-up). We took with us my good friend Virginia, and Jessica, Torrey's sister. It would be a chance for them to see first hand where Torrey and I had been during the initial visit.

We flew down the Monday morning of Thanksgiving week, arriving just in time to make the afternoon blood-pull, before checking into the Sea and Sun Manor. Since we wouldn't have a car, we wanted to be close to the IAT Centre and this place was within walking distance. It was also a place where the manager was open to having the cancer patients stay.

Torrey and I had many places that we wanted to show Jes and Virginia. Since our schedule would be pretty much the same as when we originally were there, we knew we could plan our time.

Each morning we would get up for the blood-pull at the clinic and then return to our apartment to have breakfast and sometimes a morning swim with our two guests at the pool. We would return for the shots in the late morning and then make plans for the day. We took them to the International Bazaar, to the Nature Center, and to the beach by the Holiday Inn. Our friends, Bea and Al Glander, visited us a couple of times and took us out to Harbor House to see our old apartment. It was great to see them and several friends who were back on return tune-up trips.

We also took Jes and Virginia to the IAT Centre to sit in the waiting room and meet patients so they could get the feel of the place. On the second day, we had a chance to see Dr. Burton and introduce them, and Jes got to see the mice in his research lab. I was able to get some good pictures of Torrey and Dr. Burton together. He was pleased with her new growth of red hair and laughed about his joke of telling her that her hair would come back a different color.

We met a family from New Jersey, whose son, Joey, had cancer. They were staying in the apartment next to us at the Sea and Sun. I had spoken with Joey's mom earlier in the fall when she had called to inquire about Immuno-Augmentative therapy. It was great to have the opportunity to meet her and Joey, and their family.

Thanksgiving is not observed in the Bahamas, as it is an American tradition. Some of the people in the Sea and Sun, from the States, however, were cooking turkeys. Since we were not long-term renters and equipped to cook a big dinner, we decided to go out. We had had several good breakfasts at reasonable cost at a pancake house, so we opted to try it for our dinner on Thanksgiving. We didn't have turkey, but we had delicious hamburgers and french fries. For Torrey and me the best part was having company to share the holiday.

We all missed being at home, but the week had been worth the time at the clinic. Torrey's tune-up was excellent. We had a wonderful week together and returned home with serum and a three-month shot schedule.

In January 1980, the girls had their regularly scheduled appointments with their pediatrician, and at that time Torrey was in good health. We had a white blood count done, which indicated that her blood was also fine.

We returned to Dr. Beaty's every six weeks just to keep tabs on Torrey's blood makeup by having her blood drawn and sent to the Bahamas and tested there. At the end of the three months, we got a new shot schedule. Each time we came home from a trip to Dr. Beaty's and received the message that she was in great health, we felt blessed by having found the IAT Centre in the Bahamas.

In the summer of 1980, following Torrey's year in the fifth grade, we returned to the IAT Centre for our second checkup (tune-up); our third trip to the Bahamas. This trip is reported from my diary.

Second Checkup

Monday, 6/30/80

We arrived in Freeport on the 2:00 P.M. flight. Bea was not there to meet us, so we took a taxi. We saw Dr. Burton. It was fun to see Torrey embrace him and give him a small mouse. Torrey had a blood-pull. We walked to the Sea and Sun manor where we would again be staying. Mary, Joey's mom, has reserved one of the small apartments for us on the ground floor. It is going to be very hot, as the air conditioner is broken. There were no towels, or sheets, or any kitchen equipment. I had to run down to the new manager and get what we needed. She seemed very cheerful and wanted to help us out.

We have found out that Bea is very ill. She has caught some kind of respiratory bug and apparently Al has had it too. We hope to see them this week.

The clinic is full of people, not only Americans, but Brazilians. Many of them saw the *60 Minutes* program in May 1980 on Dr. Burton and Immuno-Augmentative Therapy.

At the Sea and Sun, the patients have started a blood-pull service, which helps the clinic. Several people have volunteered to do the blood-pulls at the patients' apartments, and then someone will take all of them to the clinic to be processed. The patients only have to go to get their shots or have someone pick them up.

We have not met Amber and her mom yet, from Milford, Connecticut, or Mr. Cafferty from Branford.

Tuesday, 7/1/80

We got settled in late yesterday afternoon and took a swim. We met Macy, an eleven-year-old girl from Westbrook. Her granddad has been here for therapy for a brain tumor. He was the main attraction on the *60 Minutes* program with Dr. Burton. Her mom, Arla Amara, is helping in the clinic. She and her husband have set up the blood-pull room here at the Sea and Sun.

Tor and I sat in the clinic this morning, hoping to see Bea, but we missed her. She was to come for a late afternoon appointment, but we missed her again. We learned that Charlie Smith, our friend from Ohio, was back for a tune-up. We missed him by two weeks. He is apparently doing well.

We met Amber and her mom. She is four years old and so precious. She is bald, as Torrey was. Her mom has taught her how to give herself the shots.

We saw Mr. Cafferty. What a lovely man. He gave me a kiss and thanked me for helping him come to Freeport. I believe God brought him and I guess maybe I need to be more willing to share with others.

Torrey and I began a Bible study on 1 John today. We are

61

reading the verses and then answering some study questions together.

We hope it rains again tonight as it did yesterday. It helped keep us cool. Torrey had four shots today.

Wednesday, 7/2/80

Torrey and I played backgammon until 11:15 P.M. We thought it was only 10:00 P.M. Our little travel clock had stopped. It was so hot and sticky, but we did get to sleep. There were some palmettos crawling around.

Tor had her blood drawn at the Sea and Sun, and we met several new patients while waiting in line. We walked over to the Caffertys and they have invited us for dinner tomorrow evening. We picked up shots at the clinic and I signed up to give blood. She has four shots.

We spent the morning swimming, sunning, playing backgammon, and reading books. We took Macy with us to Kentucky Fried Chicken for dinner and then they went to *The Muppet Movie* with Amber and her mom.

I called to confirm our plane reservation for Saturday.

Thursday, 7/3/80

It was a rainy day. It seems to be the rainy season, and it is a relief. I got caught in a downpour on the way to the clinic. Tor and I chanced showers in the late morning to walk to the International Bazaar. We bought gifts for her Grandmother Morse, Evelyn, and Jes. We went to our favorite ice cream shop for a rum raisin ice-cream cone.

Our visit and dinner with the Caffertys was really special. Eva is a dear person. She and Frank are good people. They only live ten minutes from us in Connecticut. We met some of the patients at Windsor House where they are staying. Later Tor and I took a swim and did our Bible study.

We went to the clinic this morning for the blood-pull and stayed to see Dr. B. after he finished in the lab. He will see us tomorrow before we leave to give us our new shot schedule and serum. What a dear man! He always looks forward to seeing us, especially Torrey. He gave her a big hug. She gave him a wooden mouse to add to the collection. We got the shots and spent the afternoon at the pool with a picnic lunch. We listened to stories of new patients who are also staying here, particularly their cancer experiences.

When we found out that Bea was going to be at the clinic, we took the chance to get to see her. We saw her only briefly. She does not look good. That "bug" did its work.

We had a late supper, talked to Amber's mom, and read our Scriptures before turning in.

We are sitting at the airport waiting for our flight. We shared a taxi with some people from New Jersey.

We started our day late and went to the clinic for our serum to bring home and a brief chat with Dr. B. He is very pleased with Torrey's progress. He wants us back for a tune-up in six months.

The next five months were uneventful other than living our normal lives. Torrey and Jes went to Camp Washington, an

Episcopal Church Camp, during August. Torrey had been taking several shots a day, so we called Dr. Beaty and asked what we should do. We were able to let her skip shots for that week. No problems occurred.

In October, we were all excited because Dr. Burton came to visit Quinnipiac College in New Haven for a lecture, question-and-answer seminar. Torrey was thrilled to have the chance to see him away from the clinic and to take her dad, her sister, Grandmother Morse, and various support friends to meet and hear him speak.

During the week of November 23, 1980, Torrey and I were again in Freeport, Bahamas.

Monday, 11/23/80

We arrived on the 12:30 P.M. flight, in time to make the afternoon blood-pull and check in at the Sea and Sun Manor. We picked up shots late in the day and talked with several returnees. It felt good to see friends from other times and to know they were doing well.

We enjoyed a late afternoon snack of popcorn, apple juice, and carrots. We didn't buy groceries because I had brought several dried foods, tea, coffee, etc., in my suitcase. We are slowly learning the routine of tune-up visits. It seems that each time we come other patients give us new and different ideas about what to bring, etc.

We played backgammon and read.

Tuesday, 11/24/80

We were up early to make blood-pull at the clinic. When we picked up shots, we found that Tor had a note asking her to return in the afternoon for another blood-pull. I couldn't imagine why since this had not happened except one other occasion in 1979. I was sure there had to be a good reason, but I felt concerned. I intended to ask when we returned at 2:30 P.M. for the blood-pull. No one was available. When we came to pick up the second set of shots, Dr. Burton was there to talk to. My fears were relieved when he reassured me that Torrey was fine. But since she was only here for the five days, he wanted to give her immune system extra build-up. We took a few moments to visit the mice.

We met a new little boy, Gavin, from Rhode Island. He has leukemia. He is here with his mom and dad and sister. We knew they would be here because a friend of mine from Madison, Janet Wieglgus, had told us before we came. We had hoped to meet them and were pleased that they are also staying at the Sea and Sun.

Torrey is going to a birthday party for Gavin tomorrow and is excited about doing something different and having a chance to be with other folk. It makes such a difference to know others and to share a common bond with them, when you are in a place so far away from home.

Torrey and I still do not like being alone, in spite of the other trips we have made. The last two were better, since we had company. This one is hard because it is a holiday back home. I wonder how many more trips we will have to make?

I went up to the third floor to visit some new people from New Jersey and a couple from Connecticut.

Wednesday, 11/25/80

No more shots! Tor and I are in shock! We saw Dr. B. this morning. He says we don't need to stay and should be able to go tomorrow. Torrey is great! I can't believe it! Yes, I can. I just was not expecting this wonderful news! He says we can go home without serum maintenance and/or shot schedule. In other words, she is off the therapy! Torrey is so excited! She keeps telling everyone we see, "No more shots!" Truly, **a miracle** has occurred!

I called the airport. We can't go until Friday . . . something to do with the way our tickets are arranged. We are disappointed, but can't help rejoicing in our good news! Whit and Jes, everyone at home will be so happy and so thankful! "Thank you, Jesus!"

We have been invited to have Thanksgiving Day dinner with our New Jersey friends and others from the States. **What a day!!**

Thursday, 11/26/80

What a truly joyful Thanksgiving for us!!! Torrey is riding high with her news. We had a special visit with the Knotts, Ropers, Grabers, and others. Each family brought something to share so that we enjoyed quite a feast.

One young woman in her twenties came with her father and sister. She is in very bad condition from all the chemotherapy that she has had for over two years. She was in a wheelchair. I wanted to cry for her. And yet, she had such a joyous spirit and seemed to encourage us all. This seems to be the way of the cancer victim . . . encouraging those of us who are well. I was glad we could be with friends for this special day.

Torrey and I have so much to be grateful for! God is good!

We are on our way home, rejoicing in our fantastic news! No serum. Unbelievable! Yet, not so . . . !

We are sad too. The young woman we met at dinner yesterday died this morning. My heart aches for her family. It was too late for her to come. Soon we will be home.

(11:00 P.M.)

Whitney and Jessica welcomed us home. We will celebrate Torrey's end of IAT shots with Grandmom Morse on the weekend. We are still all in wonderful shock. . . . Torrey has come to the end of the regular therapy! Yes! **A marvelous miracle has taken place for Torrey and in our lives! God, I thank you!**

In July 1981, Torrey and I returned to the IAT clinic for her semi-annual tune-up. Whit and Jessica went along. We had an enjoyable week, showing them all of the sights of the island that we had discovered in our several visits.

We returned to the States for a four-day respite at Disney World in Florida. Once again, we returned home without serum maintenance. We expected this to be the result, but it was still a wonder to us!!

When Tor and I checked into the clinic, six months later, November 1981, Dr. Burton was ready to send us home after two days. Torrey's immune system seems to be holding its own. We were able to get a flight out and make it home late Thanksgiving night. No maintenance, and this time instructions to come back in a year.

In 1982 while in Freeport for a five day tune-up, Torrey and I were interviewed by Renee Ackerman, reporter for the *Freeport News*, Freeport. The following is a copy of that interview.

'I Am So Grateful We Found Dr. Burton and Grand Bahama Island'
Renee Ackerman

She was eight years old and had her tonsils removed in September 1978. Two weeks later Margaret Morse discovered a small flap where the left tonsil had been in her daughter Torrey's throat. In only two days time the flap grew to the size of a thumb. Mrs. Morse brought her daughter back to the surgeon who immediately placed Torrey in the hospital and removed the growth. It proved malignant. The diagnosis: HISTIOCYTIC LYMPHOMA.

★   ★   ★

"Torrey was put through a regimen of chemotherapy for four months," her mother reported, "during which time she lost all her hair, she was very ill . . . throwing up all the time and her entire body was bloated. They were giving her seven different chemo drugs.

"The doctors recommended cranial radiation and three years of chemotherapy. Torrey was so frightened every time she went for a treatment I said 'no way.' In February 1979, Torrey developed the flu and the chemo stopped. Torrey never went back on it again."

Mrs. Morse brightened.

"A friend at church suggested we look into alternative therapy. She suggested we see a certain doctor in Cos Cob, Connecticut, who suggested Dr. Lawrence Burton and his immunotherapy in the Bahamas. The fact Immuno Augmen-

tative Therapy is nontxoic we felt even if we came to Freeport and the therapy didn't work we weren't hurting her.

"Everything fell into place. I got the leave of absence from school I needed, we found the money to pay for the trip. It was just meant to be," she said.

"We left our Guilford, Connecticut, home March 16 for Freeport. After the first three weeks we noticed a marked improvement in Torrey. She

Torrey, age 9, May 1979.

68

lost the bloatedness, her hair started to grow back, she regained her strength. She was a healthy little girl. After five and one-half weeks we left the Immunology Researching Centre with serum and were home for Easter.

"We were back and forth for checkups and in November 1980, Dr. Burton pronounced Torrey cured. She was taken off the IAT injections at home and we were told she didn't have to return to Freeport for six months. She has been leading a perfectly normal active life. She is in the eighth grade in school, and hasn't missed a day. The only time she missed school was when she was on chemotherapy.

"The last time we were here was November 1981, when Dr. Burton told us Torrey wouldn't need a checkup for one year. Torrey will be thirteen years old December 14 and we expect to go home for another year without home maintenance. She takes shots while she is here in Freeport just to make sure. But, she is free of cancer."

I RECOMMEND

Mrs. Morse was smiling.

"I recommend IAT to everyone," she said, "but you can't pressure people. At least they should know about this."

Torrey added, "Dr. Burton is a kind and generous man. I think he is fantastic."

When asked their feelings about Freeport, Mrs. Morse replied, "If you have to leave home for treatment, this is the best place I can think of. The beaches are the best I've ever seen. Most people I've met here have been very nice. I am so grateful we found Dr. Burton and Grand Bahama Island."

(*Freeport News*, November 1982. Reprinted with permission by the *Nassau Guardian* DBA the *Freeport News*.)

For several years, Torrey returned to the IAT Centre in Freeport, Grand Bahama Island, Bahamas, with me for her tune-up, knowing that she was fine. She always got shots during the tune-up week. On some of those trips, we took part of our family or different friends with us so they could share the experience with us and enjoy the island.

In recent years, Torrey has returned either once every year or two with her sister as a companion and/or with a friend.

Torrey graduated in the top ten percent of her Guilford High School class in 1987. She played saxophone in the marching, concert, and jazz bands, participated as a member of the junior and varsity volleyball teams, and on the varsity track team, throwing the javelin and discus. She played, as

69

well, on several town recreational softball teams. She spent a year as an AFS (American Field Service) exchange student in Brazil after high school and spent her junior year of college in Latin America, a semester in Ecuador and a semester in Guatemala and Colombia. She is a Latin American Studies graduate from the University of Vermont and is now working toward a master's degree in counseling. Torrey is at present a vocational rehabilitation counselor with the State of Connecticut Bureau of Rehabilitation Services in New Haven, Connecticut.

8

Spiritual Journey

1 Corinthians 13:7: **Love bears all things, believes all things, hopes all things, endures all things.**

My husband Whit and I believe that Torrey's excellent health and good quality of life are God's work and that Dr. Burton's Immuno-Augmentative Therapy was the instrument, along with the power of prayer for healing.

From all of my life experience right up to this point in time, I have come to believe that life is a journey, and this journey is toward God. As we move toward God, we are able to find the God within who moves and guides our souls. I have come to know that each day the decisions we make are choices made either out of love or out of fear. It is such a simple concept, but one I would not have been able to state back when Torrey was first ill. However, it is my belief that the choices my husband, Whit, and I made during that period came from that concept: Love or Fear.

I know that for us to risk all: making a decision to try an alternative therapy, one not even found in our own country; leaving our doctors at Yale New Haven Hospital and the American medical establishment's method of treatment; my taking time from my job for several weeks without pay; calling on others to help us financially; my leaving Whit to care for Jessica and having to rely on family and friends to care for her while he was at work; none of these were easy choices.

We knew that the medical establishment would not be happy with us, but we went ahead. These choices did not come easily. But Love, love for our precious daughter, love that only God can give, helped us make those most important decisions. Love gave us the courage. Love nurtured us, comforted us, inspired and taught us. And at the end, this same Love will call us home. Love, for God is love.

In the next several pages, I wish to give some insight as to what took place in our lives concerning faith, faith (belief) in God, during this whole process of Torrey's illness and searching for another treatment.

Early on when Torrey was still receiving chemotherapy and we were seeing no results, just a daughter who was physically deteriorating before our eyes, we did a lot of questioning . . . questioning God, asking the why questions . . . Why Torrey? Why our family? What did we do? Why a child? etc.

My sister, Barbara, and her husband, Richard, had lost their son, Bob, to this dreaded disease in 1974. His diagnosis was leukemia. He was their only child. I could not imagine losing a child. But they did and I know that it was their faith that carried them through. I even remember saying to Barbara, once, on a visit to their home in California, "How did you do it? How did you walk through Bob's illness? I couldn't." But they did. Their faith carried them through Bob's illness and his death. I believe it is because they knew they couldn't bear it. But they knew God would bear it for them. God carried them through the illness of their son and through his death.

And God was with us, as well, through all of Torrey's illness.

It was just four years later when our young daughter was diagnosed with cancer, and both Whit and I knew deep within each of our beings that God would carry us through no matter what.

This would not be the first time. Two years before, our

younger child, Jessica, had suffered a severe head injury due to a fall from her bike. Though the stay in the hospital was only several days, a small five-year-old child is very delicate. This kind of injury might have had terrible after effects on our very precious child and on all our lives.

We knew the power of prayer from this incident and we believe, having walked through both a serious head injury with one child and a devastating disease with the other, that both of our daughters are gifts to us . . . gifts to us, twice over through their birth to us and then by the healing that occurred for each of them.

During this period of our lives with Torrey's illness, our friends, family, and the people in our church, Christ Episcopal Church, Guilford, Connecticut, were very supportive and were continually praying for Torrey's wellness and strength for our family.

Right at the start, when Torrey's second surgery had been done and the surgeon had come to tell us that a growth had been removed but was malignant, our priest, the Rev. Bradford Locke, and one of our dear friends, Worth Cox, arrived on the scene. Whit and I stood in the hallway of St. Raphael's Hospital devastated by the news. These two men arrived within seconds of each other. Both over six feet tall, large men, they embraced us as we literally fell into their arms. We felt the love, God's love through their comforting arms.

Early on during the chemotherapy and with the knowledge of possible radiation, our local druggist, Dick Dudley, and our dentist, Dr. Small, came to the forefront. They donated an electric waterpick for Torrey. They knew that keeping Torrey's teeth and mouth in good condition was going to be essential. Later when we chose the IAT alternative therapy, Dick Dudley came through again, donating syringes to us for her injections. These were acts of love!

In trying to search my memory of this period of our lives,

I searched for and I found all the cards that were sent to Torrey and to our family, all from those same people and from her fourth-grade classmates.

On January 4, 1998, as I sat with my husband looking through these cards, it was interesting how many of them brought out the faith they were expressing for healing from God and/or encouraging us to look to God for healing. We read them and once more tears came to our eyes even after almost twenty years. Expressions of faith such as, "God bless you, my prayers are that you will be well soon." "God keep you and bless you," "Get well soon. And, I hope you feel better." "God protect you." "Trust the Lord always." "Our prayers are with you and we know that Jesus is with you and has put his healing hand upon you. God bless you." "God is with you." "Love and prayers."

A card sent from her sister, Jessica, age seven, expressed her love, a love that God gives for a sister. It was a picture with little orange-and-red hearts that she had drawn and that said, "I love you, Torrey, Jessica."

Later as Torrey was obviously better and on a healing path, cards came that expressed the happiness and joy people felt for her healing, but also most of them gave the appropriate recognition to God for his hand in it all. "We heard the good news, that God is taking control. Praise the Lord"; "We've been praying and trusting you will soon be home and back in school. God is good and he loves you very much. Trust him," "We thank God for keeping you in his hand." And on and on.

These cards with expressions of faith and the prayers of so many family and friends within our community and spread around the country kept us knowing that God would be there for us. But we had to believe it and we did.

A dear college friend and her husband, Judy and Fran Barillaro, had traveled to Rome and to the Chapel of St. Fran-

This card, filled with "God's love," was given by seven-year-old Jessica to her older sister Torrey in 1979.

cis of Assisi during the fall of 1978, and while there, they gave Torrey's name for special prayers.

Friends in our community and from around the country were holding Torrey up to God for healing.

One very significant event occurred in November of 1978, during the period when Torrey was on chemotherapy. It is one that I believe gave Torrey's dad Whitney and me the courage to make our eventual decision to change treatment and take Torrey out of the United States. It was a healing service. I had been told of this service by the church secretary, Stella Woodworth.

This healing service took place at the Connecticut Valley (Whiting Institute) Hospital in Middletown, Connecticut, on a Sunday night. An Anglican priest, visiting in this country from Great Britain, a man who himself had been healed from mental illness, was conducting his last service there before returning to England. I called a couple of my friends, Virginia Cox and Juanita Gerkin, and they made arrangements to go with me. This service was one of powerful emotion and a very different experience for me.

"O Love that casts out fear . . . tarry no more with out, but come and dwell within" (Horatius Bonar [1808–1889]).

Though I had been to a variety of teaching services and healing prayer services, I had never actually gone up to the front and had someone lay hands on me. I had always been an observer. And, though I was a believer in such healing prayer, I had never risked going forward. I was encouraged to do this and I was fearful. But in the end, out of love, I went up. The priest laid his hands on me, not even knowing why I was there or whom I wanted prayers for. He touched my forehead and said some words . . . words I don't even remember. But I fell backward and lay on the floor. Within myself, I was embarrassed, but I knew I had had a wonderful and blessed thing happen to me.

It was because of this experience during this service that I became convinced that Torrey would be all right. I did not know how or when or what would occur for this to happen, but I was given the message and conviction through this powerful meeting, that this illness was not going to take her life. I went home knowing this. However, having this conviction did not mean that as a mother I did not give up my concern or have fearful days, but deep inside I knew.

People were sent into our lives throughout Torrey's treatment at the hospital to spell us when we needed it. Friends who sat with me while she had chemotherapy: Harriet Sayre, Virginia Cox; and Evelyn Linskey, who gave me great comfort after each session. They did this out of their love, a love that only God can give for a friend.

One of the occurrences that I think illustrates the way the children cared for Torrey, besides sending her cards, was when she was wearing her wig.

Torrey was in the fourth grade at the time of her illness. After she had started chemotherapy, she had told the kids in her class that her hair was going to fall out. In her concern for them, she took the wig to school and showed it to the class. She explained the netting underneath that helps the scalp breathe. She told them that one day she would have her own hair and the next day she would come in with a wig. And in actuality this is what happened. All of her hair fell out in one night. After this terrible falling out of hair, Torrey was wearing her wig to school daily.

A fellow teacher related this incident to me. At noontime recess Torrey liked to play basketball with the boys. One day while they were playing, her wig fell off. There was no chuckling or embarrassment, except Torrey's. The boys, Scott, Dan R., Dan F., boys from her class and others, gathered around her, making a protective wall, hiding her from other children on the playground. She picked up her wig, put it back on, and they continued their game.

The little girls in the Brownie Troop that she was in were very compassionate in the way they treated her as well.

These incidents illustrate Torrey's concern for her classmates and theirs for her, as she walked through her illness. Their action and hers were acts made out of love. Acts, I believe, of God's love.

Whit and I observed her faith grow during this time. She seemed to grow in her understanding of the teachings of Jesus she had in Sunday school and discussions we had at home. I saw a trust in her of us, her parents, that was firm. She did not seem afraid of the possibility of dying. A good friend had given us a book on death written for children, *If I Should Die, If I*

Should Live, by Joanna Benjamin Marxhauser. We read it to both the girls and it seemed very helpful.

The night Whit and I made the decision to try this alternative therapy, we lay in our bed trying to figure out how it would all work. We were both emotionally drained. How would we pay for this treatment? Who would care for Jessica? As we lay there, I remember Whit crying and tearfully saying to me, "How will we do it? Where will we get the money to do this?" I know that God's love convinced the people who offered and/or gave us money so that we could go. We had not asked for any help. People literally left money in our mail box. Friends gave us financial help. My parents, already retired, lent us money as well. One of my brothers-in-law, Dean Buckley, offered financial help. We, Whit and I, believe that God took care of our financial needs and all of our needs at that time.

I believe that it was God who opened the doors for us to find the way to an alternative treatment for Torrey. I believe it was God's grace that allowed me to get permission from the Board of Education and acting superintendent Nils Peterson to leave my job for those several weeks in order to go with Torrey to the IAT Centre in the Bahamas. And when I returned home, though I had not expected to be paid, all of my pay checks were there. This had to be an act of God. Even when I questioned this occurrence and tried to return the checks, I was told they were mine to keep.

When going to the Bahamas, we needed to get records and copies of all the tests that Torrey had undergone at the hospital, as well as what chemotherapy she had taken up to this point. This was a touchy situation because we really didn't know how doctors or the hospital personnel would act and/or react to our leaving the established method of treatment. We already knew that our pediatrician did not approve of our plans. We did not want to leave the hospital on bad terms, and we were appreciative of their efforts. We truly felt that our on-cologist and other medical staff who had worked with Torrey cared for her and that they believed they were doing the best possible treatment for her.

At that point in time, it was difficult to get records, but God provided. With the help of one of the residents, we were able to get all the necessary papers without any difficulty.

God knows that we do not always trust as we should and knows that we often need assurance. Once Torrey and I got to the Bahamas, we did need it.

And God once more gave us courage and trust. When we arrived at the clinic the first time, we met other patients and their families, all of whom had come believing and knowing that at this place there was a new and different kind of survival. The IAT Centre was not like the hospital at home where there was a dread of this disease and of the eventual outcome which we all knew . . . death. Death either from the disease or from the treatment. In the hospital at home there was that particular smell . . . a smell of medicine and death, which was not found in this place.

In the IAT Centre in Freeport, there was a clean smell, and a great feeling throughout of hope in healing. We met peo-ple of faith, people who had also come because they believed God had opened doors for them . . . had shown them this path.

Each morning in the waiting area, patients and family members shared their stories of coming to this place of hope. In all of my conversations with Dr. Burton, a man of the Jewish faith, he always gave credit to God for this treatment.

It was into our third week in the Bahamas after Torrey and I moved into our own apartment at the Harbor House when we received a knock at our door. The young woman, Mrs. Shultz, a maid for our neighbor and a native of the island, stood there. We had seen her previously only to say hello. She had heard of Torrey and her illness. She wanted us to come to a healing serv-

Dr. Burton and Torrey, age 12, in 1982.

ice. See how God works? I needed reassurance. She stepped back from me even as she asked, because of her own fear that Torrey's disease might be catching. After my convincing her that this was not the case, she was more comfortable. She wanted us to come on the following Thursday to the weekly prayer and healing service at the Church of the God of Prophecy at noontime. I told her that I had no way of getting to her church, which was out at the west end of the island. She encouraged us to come and said that she and her husband would pick us up. She would be meet us outside on Thursday at 11:00 A.M. "Please come." She left with the question left unanswered.

I didn't know what to think. Should I go and take Torrey? Who was this woman? Once again God gave me help. In the mail the next day a letter from my friend, Virginia, came. It was a regular letter, but at the end, she wrote this sentence as a P.S. "Margaret, you may have to do things that you may not want to." God knew I was fearful of going with Mrs. Shultz. But this message, from Virginia, which she told me later she doesn't remember writing, gave me courage to take Torrey and go.

Torrey and I went with this family in their battered station wagon out to Eight Mile Rock. We went into a building that was painted a bright pink and filled with several hundred Bahamians sitting on or standing in front of old wooden pews. Torrey and I were the only Caucasian people. The service was strange and emotional, but a wonderful experience.

At first I felt frightened, but then the enthusiasm of these native island people, in their way of worship and the compassion they gave to us, put me at ease. Torrey, I knew, was feeling a little scared.

The service began with introductory words from the elder in charge. The pastor was away, off the island at a conference. There was singing and praying. Praying of a kind that I was not used to, being from America and a conservative/formal type of worship background. These people prayed aloud, all at the same time, waving their hands, shouting their praises and needs. I was uncomfortable at first. But the Spirit, I believe, both Torrey and I felt, took care of any fear or discomfort.

At some point the healing portion of the service took place. The elders, of whom there were twelve, I assume like the twelve apostles, stood up in two lines of six, facing one another about four feet apart.

The congregation was asked if there was anyone who wished healing. A number of persons began going forward and going through this line. The elders would lay hands on them and shout out prayers over them . . . Ms. Shultz encouraged me to take Torrey up. I did. We walked together through the line. Each elder placed his hands on each of our heads, pushing down in a rough way, but with such fervency of faith that it was okay. Each one prayed loud and long over us, asking for healing and God's mercy. At the end of the line, the elder, who was in charge of the service, anointed us with holy oil. He gave me the bottle to take so I could continue anointing Torrey.

These people wanted Torrey and me to share our story. They wanted to hear of our faith experience. I was in awe of their faith! How would I be able to tell our experience? Speak of my faith? But again, God helped us through. Both Torrey and I spoke.

From this most incredible experience, my faith was once again confirmed of Torrey's eventual wellness and healing. Yes, for the next two years, as long as Torrey was taking injections, I held concern, as a mother does. But I knew she would be fine and know so even to this day. I continued to anoint her daily with that oil.

While Torrey and I were in Freeport for the initial stay, we attended a Scottish Presbyterian Church (Kirk). The Celtic cross, a giant towering stone structure outside the church, always impressed me. My background, as a child, was Presbyterian and it was a joy to me to have that cross remind me of my faith.

Once, while we were attending services at this Presbyterian Kirk, a brush fire took place and swept right past the building. We could see it come and move right up to the building, to the windows, and then pass over us. Though I knew the building was fireproof and the preacher reassured the congregation of our safety even as he preached while the fire came, both Torrey and I were awed. This incident just deepened my awareness of God in our lives on this small island far away from home.

In our beginning weeks staying with our friends Bea and Al Glander, we went to their place of worship, the Seventh-

Day Adventist Church. Their Sabbath is Saturday and so those weekends we went twice to church.

We also went to Christ the King Church (Anglican) near the Centre. We went here because at home in Connecticut we attend the Episcopal Church whose tradition stems from the Anglican Church, the Church of England. We liked the music there. Having sung in choirs all my life and having directed two children's choirs, I was inspired by the way the Bahamians sang. The hymns were sung with faithful enthusiasm. All the psalm responses were sung. You knew on hearing them that they believed the words that they were singing. There was a rhythm to the voices that was impressive. The pronunciation and accent of words were staccato and clear. This was true of the whole congregation, not just a few.

The organist at this church was a young girl of fourteen. She had a real gift. My understanding, from what we were told, was that she came from a family of talented musicians. We tried to get to the service early so we could hear her practice the hymns and listen to any other musicians practicing. Sometimes there would be instruments played during the service or just before. We always went away from the worship filled with joy and a new hope in God.

All of our experiences in worshiping were different but special in the acknowledgment of God in our lives.

One of the things that Torrey and I began doing early on was reading the Bible each day and studying the Scriptures concerning baptism. Many churches baptize by immersion, usually when the child is ten to twelve, old enough to make his or her own decision. In our Episcopal tradition, baptism is done by sprinkling when the child is a baby and at the parents' discretion. In many traditions it is known as being christened. It is my understanding in this present time that the Episcopal Church will immerse if the person so chooses.

Bea and Al, Torrey and I would have religious discussions. One concerned the understanding and purpose of baptism. In our study of the Scriptures, Torrey and I decided that we wanted to be baptized by immersion.

We both were already baptized through sprinkling: I through the choice of my parents and Torrey through the choice of her dad and me. We felt, however, that we wanted to make this reaffirmation of our faith. I believe we were convinced (led) through our study of Scripture, prayer, and discernment to make this decision.

Torrey and I, firm in our decision, persevered and were baptized by immersion after we returned to the United States and Guilford. We had a friend of our family, the Rev. Martin Van Horn do this second baptism. It was done in the Hammonasett River, Madison, Connecticut, in June 1979. I believe there was a quality of healing in this decision by us. It was because we chose to commit ourselves to belief in God, in front of family and friends, through the same act that Jesus had made as an adult. We were not rejecting the faith of our parents, but claiming our own belief. It was another assurance of faith for her and me.

The Scripture we used the most, daily, was Psalm 103. Before Torrey and I left Connecticut to fly to the Bahamas, my friend Virginia had given us this Scripture:

Bless the Lord, O my soul,
and all that is within me, bless his Holy name.
Bless the Lord, O my soul,
and forget not all his benefits.
He forgives all your sins
and heals all your infirmities;
He redeems your life from the grave,
and crowns you with mercy and loving kindness;
He satisfies you with good things,
and your youth is renewed like an eagle's.

—Psalm 103:1–5

Virginia's recommendation was to say it every day, even memorize it. Torrey and I used these first five verses to memorize and say this each morning. It was discipline for us and one I learned to cherish doing. These words gave us grounding for each day during that critical period of our lives. When I look at these verses today, I see that they also give us the truth of how we are to live our lives.

We don't always make the right choices in our humanness. But, I firmly believe that all of our choices come out of our faith from the God within the very core of our being. "Bless the Lord, O my soul and all that is within me, bless his holy name." Or, they come from fear and our ego. I have come to know that if we listen to the Greater Self, to that "still small voice" within our soul, we can make the right choices, choices that come out of Love. I believe that through God's grace and mercy Whit and I were able to make the decisions we did for Torrey, out of Love. And, God is LOVE!

Postscript

Torrey was given the IAT therapy with daily injections from March 1979 through November 1981. After the initial five and a half weeks as an outpatient at the IAT Centre, she was given this therapy at home. She returned to the Centre in Freeport every six months for a five-day tune-up and monitoring through daily blood-pulls.

Following November 1981 she was taken off the injections, except for each return trip every six months for five days for the next two years. In 1983 she began going back just once a year. During the five-day tune-up, as it is called, she received injections to boost her immune system.

This therapy has never had any side effects on Torrey, except for occasional tiredness in the initial weeks. We have never seen any or heard of any side effects in any of our patient friends except for occasional tiredness in older patients.

In 1983, Dr. Burton was researching a treatment for AIDS (Acquired Immune Deficiency Syndrome), which had become a major problem in the United States. In his research he discovered that the syndrome is not due to bacteria or virus, but something suppressing the immune system and allowing normal bacteria and virus, that a healthy individual can throw off, to grow and kill the person. Burton said, "I am looking for the immune suppression. This is a link between the immune mechanism in AIDS and the immune mechanism in cancer. But it is pure theory" (Thurston, 1983).

Burton reports success in treating two AIDS victims using the same treatment given to cancer patients only in a much lower and less aggressive dose. It boosted their immune systems and alleviated their symptoms. However, the patients are still on medication. Burton does not know what will happen if they stop and they haven't wanted to stop (Morse, 1984).

In 1985, the IAT Centre was closed down by the Bahamian Health Officials.

The reasons for the Clinic's closure were unclear, but were soon known to center around the charge that a "health hazard" existed due to the alleged presence of antibodies to the AIDS virus in the serums being used for treatment at the Clinic. The charge was later found to be fraudulently fabricated by U.S. health authorities who had long been searching for any excuse to pressure the Bahamian government to close the Freeport Clinic (IATPA, 1988).

Due to this dark day for IAT patients, two patients, Jack Link and A.T. LaPrade joined with Nat Owen, husband of patient Janet Owen, to seek and obtain incorporation of the IAT Patients' Association (IATPA) as a tax-exempt public benefit corporation under IRS provisions 501(C) (3).

The fighting spirit of the patients and families rallied during that period and the first major action of *IAT Patients' Association* was initiated. Torrey and our family joined them in a march on Washington and visits with members of Congress. The Centre was reopened.

This association exists today under the name *People Against Cancer* for the purpose of advocating a number of cancer treatments.

In 1988, a team of researchers from the University of Pennsylvania led by cancer researcher, Barrie Cassileth, Ph.D., conducted a small retrospective study that compared 79 people with cancer treated with IAT to 79 similar people treated with conventional therapy at the University of Pennsylvania.

The following are the results of the U of Penn Study.

37 percent of the people treated with IAT had improved performance status;

33 percent of the people treated with IAT had improved appetite and weight;

97 percent of the people treated with IAT had no side effects from treatment; and

Survival was nearly double with IAT when compared to standard treatment.

(OPTIONS, the Newsletter of People Against Cancer, p. 5, 1998.)

The Morse family in August 1996. From left to right: Torrey, dad Whitney, Jessica, and mom Margaret.

Torrey was interviewed over the phone for this study.

In November, 1997, Torrey returned to the Bahamas for her annual tune-up. Two weeks prior to her return, she had discovered an enlarged lymph node on her groin. Her medical doctor told her that it might just be some sort of infection. She chose not to do anything about it, except to have a white cell and lymph blood count done and to ask for prayers. The blood test turned out to be normal, and the node had disappeared before she got to the IAT Centre.

While she was at the IAT Centre, her daily blood test continually showed very high tumor kill and irregular response to the shots she received. This was the first sign since her original visit to the clinic of any irregular activity in her immune system. As a result she stayed for a month instead of her usual one week. There was the question of recurrence. On December 5, 1997, Torrey returned home as usual without treatment, but with the request to return not in a year, but in six months for two weeks.

When Torrey talked to her dad and heard my obvious concern regarding her need to extend her stay, her response to us was, "Mom, Dad, you shouldn't worry. Worrying will not help. If there is anything to be concerned about, I am in the right place. I will be fine, it is in God's hands." So we did. And yes, she was in the right place! Torrey returned to her job, which had not been in jeopardy. She continues to be in good health.

In June 1998, she returned to the IAT Centre for two weeks. She received her tune up and returned home in good health. She plans to return in a year.

"So faith, hope, love abide, these three; but the greatest of these is love" *(I Corinthians 13:13).*

Conclusion: Spring 1998

Cancer is a devastating disease. It penetrates not only the lives of its victims, but the lives of their families and caring friends around them. It carries its pain physically to the patients, and emotionally to all concerned. Life in the family of a cancer victim becomes one of worry and emotional upheaval, along with a whole new routine centered around treatment schedules. The treatment often becomes a horror and occasionally it becomes the killer. Our family walked through the cancer experience and found a therapy that gave success. It is my hope that all who have read this story will be encouraged in their faith and in the knowledge that there are a variety of methods available for the treatment of cancer, both traditional and untraditional. It is my hope that choices when made, can be made out of love, rather than fear.

Torrey, 1998

There is choice
in all decisions!

Torrey 11/2005

Appendix

Available Alternatives

IAT (Immuno-Augmentative Therapy) Centre, Freeport
Grand Bahama Island, Bahamas,
Dr. R. John Clement, Medical Director
1-242-352-7455 FAX: 1-242-352-3201
WEB http://www.iatclinic.com

Burzynski Clinic
12000 Richmond Suite
Houston, TX 77082-2431
1-713-597-0111

Essiac: An herbal treatment purchased through Nutri-
  Care
1-888-688-9922

Cell Specific Cancer Therapy (CSCT) A Biomagnetic
  Cancer Therapy (Information can be gotten from
  the People Against Cancer Organization listed be-
  low.)

For other alternatives, write to or fax or E-mail:

People Against Cancer
PO Box 10
Otho, Iowa 50569
FAX: 1-515-972-4415
E-mail: nocancer@ix.netcom.com
WEB: http://www.dodgenet.com/nocancer

References

Ackerman, Renee. "I am so grateful we found Dr. Burton and Grand Bahama Island," *Freeport News*, 1982.

American Cancer Society. *Cancer Facts and Figures*. New York, 1979. (ACS's *Cancer Facts and Figures* is routinely published in the year before the cover date; e.g., the above volume was actually published in 1978. To avoid confusion, the fact books are listed according to the year to which they refer on the cover.)

Bonar, Horatius. 'O Love that Casts Out Fear,' p. 700 *The Hymnal 1982* Accompaniment Edition, volume 2 according to the use of the Episcopal Church, the Church Hymnal Corporation.

IAT (Bahamas) Ltd. Booklet, 1996 (pp.1, 2, & 3).

IAT Patients Association. *History of the IAT Patients' Association*. IATPA, Otho, Iowa, May 1988.

Morse, Torrey P. "IAT: Immuno-Augmentative Therapy," English II-1, November 26, 1984.

Moss, Ralph W. "The Proven Methods," *The Cancer Syndrome*. New York: Grove City Press, 1980.

Options, the Newsletter of People Against Cancer, Volume 4, Number 1, March 1998.

Psalm 103, *The Oxford Annotated Bible with the Apocrypha Revised Standard Version*, New York: Oxford University Press, 1977.

Thurston, Gladstone. "AIDS Treatment Breakthrough at Freeport Cancer Centre," *Freeport News*, XXIII–189, August 16, 1983.

Waldron, James A., M.D. *Pathology Report*, Yale New Haven Hospital, October 13, 1978.